DIRECTOR'S GUIDE

ALL YOU NEED TO PLAN YOUR VBS!

REPRODUCIBLE! INCLUDES CD-ROM

CONTENTS

Gospel Light's 2007 VBS 4
Dear Director 5
   Here's What's New! 5
   Expand Your VBS 5

Exciting theme!

SonForce Kids Course Overview 6
Curriculum Ordering Guide 8
Snapshot of SonForce Kids 9
   Course Description 9
   Set the Atmosphere 9
   Bonus Theme Ideas 10
Materials Preview 14
   Starter Kit 14
   Director's Sample Pack 14
   Super Decorating & Resource Pack 16
   Music & Skit Production Pack 16
   Super Starter Pack 16

First time as a VBS Director? Look here to get started!

Step-by-Step Planning Guide 17

1. **PLAN** 18
   Choose Your Format 18
   Choose Your Learning Plan 19
   Planning Your Early Childhood VBS 20
   Director's Calendar 22
   How to Expand to a 10-Day VBS 24

2. **RECRUIT** 26
   Assessing Your Personnel Needs 26
   Guidelines for Success 26
   Staffing Needs 27
   Using Youth Helpers 29
   Sample Flyers for Staff Recruitment 30

3. **TRAIN VOLUNTEERS** 31
   Preparing for the Meetings 31
   Sample General Training Meeting 32
   Sample Age-Level Training Meeting 32
   Hints for Successful Meetings 33

4. **PUBLICIZE** 34
   Build VBS Interest Within the Church 34
   Reach Out to Children from the Community 34

5. **PREPARE FOR EVANGELISM** 35

6. **FOLLOW UP** 36
   Follow Up on Children and Families 36
   Follow Up on Administrative Issues 37
   Follow Up in Your Church 37
   Follow Up with Your Staff 37

Safety First! 39
Opening and Closing Assemblies 40
   Dropping Off 40
   Picking Up 40
Preventing Child Abuse 41
Ensuring Safety on Campus 42
   Special Safety Concerns for Early Childhood 42
Dealing with Sick or Injured Children 42

HOW TO MAKE CLEAN COPIES FROM THIS BOOK

You may make copies of portions of this book with a clean conscience if

>> you (or someone in your organization) are the original purchaser;

>> you are using the copies you make for a noncommercial purpose (such as teaching or promoting your ministry) within your church or organization;

>> you follow the instructions provided in this book.

By following these guidelines you help us keep our products affordable.
Thank you,
Gospel Light

However, it is ILLEGAL for you to make copies if

>> you are using the material to promote, advertise or sell a product or service other than for ministry fund-raising;

>> you are using the material in or on a product for sale; or

>> you or your organization are not the original purchaser of this book.

© 2007 Gospel Light, Ventura, CA 93006. All rights reserved. Printed in the U.S.A.

Fun events to get everyone in the VBS spirit!

Special Events 43
 Field Trips 44
 Events at Church 44
 Preview Event 45
 Closing Program 50

Publicity Guide 51
 Build VBS Interest Within the Church 52
 Publicity Pieces 52
 Reach Out to Children from the Community 53
 Publicity Materials 53
 Publicity Calendar 54

Keep your parents and staff up-to-date and informed!

Newsletters 55

Activity Center Guide 57
 The Activity Center Plan—How it Works 59
 Helpful Hints 59
 Diagram for Sample Activity Center Schedule 60

Missions and Service Center Guide 63
 Your VBS Missions Project 64
 Choosing a Missions Project 64
 Missions and Service Ideas 64
 Blast-Off Project 65
  Blast-Off Visual 65
  Optional Ideas 66
 Missions Activities 68

Nursery and Toddler Guide 73
 Choosing Caregivers 74
 Playtime! 74
 Teaching Tips 75
 Planning a Schedule 76
 Session 1 77
 Session 2 79
 Session 3 81
 Session 4 83
 Session 5 85

Preteen Enrichment Ideas 87

Intergenerational VBS Guide 89
 Bring Families Together 90
 How It Works 90
 Teaching Tips 93
 Schedule Options 96

Backyard Bible School Guide 97
 What It Is 98
 Facilities 98
 How It Works 98
 The Staff 98
 Backyard Bible School Calendar 100
 Sample Schedule 100

Appendices 101
 Director's Guide Index 102
 Product Index 102
 VBS Questionnaire 103

Permission to make photocopies of or to reproduce by any other mechanical or electronic means in whole or in part any designated* page, illustration or activity in this book is granted only to the original purchaser and is intended for non-commercial use within a church or other Christian organization. None of the material in this book, not even those pages with permission to photocopy, may be reproduced for any commercial promotion, advertising or sale of a product or service or to share with any other persons, churches or organizations. Sharing of the material in this book with other churches or organizations not owned or controlled by the original purchaser is also prohibited. All rights reserved.

*Do not make any copies from this book unless you adhere strictly to the guidelines found on this page. Only pages with the following notation can be legally reproduced:

© 2007 Gospel Light. Permission to photocopy granted. SonForce Kids *Director's Guide*

Gospel Light Vacation Bible School

Senior Managing Editor, Sheryl Haystead >> **Senior Editor,** Heather Kempton Wahl >> **Editor,** Karen McGraw >> **Contributing Editors,** Kim Fiano, Heather Johnston, Anne Lupo, Tammy Wise-DiPerna >> **Art Directors,** Lori Hamilton, Samantha A. Hsu, Lenndy McCullough >> **Senior Designer,** Carolyn Thomas

Founder, Dr. Henrietta Mears >> **Publisher,** William T. Greig >> **Senior Consulting Publisher,** Dr. Elmer L. Towns >> **Senior Consulting Editor,** Wesley Haystead, M.S.Ed. >> **Senior Editor, Biblical and Theological Issues,** Bayard Taylor, M.Div.

Scripture quotations are taken from the *Holy Bible, New International Version®*. Copyright © 1973, 1978, 1984 by International Bible Society. Used by permission of Zondervan Publishing House. All rights reserved.

GOSPEL LIGHT'S 2007 VBS

FROM START TO FINISH, YOU'LL FIND IT EASIER THAN EVER TO USE OUR VBS IN YOUR CHURCH.

Now Better Than Ever!

Dear Director,

Whether you're a first-year or veteran VBS director, you'll want to read this information to find out how Gospel Light has improved its VBS. Based on suggestions and feedback from churches just like yours, we've changed to save you time and effort. From start to finish, you'll find it easier than ever to use our VBS in your church—no matter which learning plan you choose.

Here's What's New!

>> Ever think one of the forms or schedules in this *Director's Guide* would be perfect if only you could make one or two small changes? Well, now you can! This year the entire *Director's Guide* is available on the *Director's Guide CD-ROM*. And a terrific assortment of forms, schedules and calendars are available in customizable formats. Throughout this guide, look for suggested ways to use the articles and forms.

>> Also available on the *Director's Guide CD-ROM* is a terrific selection of newsletters: daily newsletters for staff and daily newsletters just for parents. Customize the newsletters for your VBS.

>> As VBS Director, you're responsible for getting all the materials in the hands of the leaders and helpers who need them. Did you ever wish there was a list of all these resources and where they can be found? This year's *Director's Guide* includes an index to let you know where you can find various resources like the coloring pages and decorating information. The index is available on page 102.

>> Now you have even more options for customizing your opening and closing assemblies to suit your staff, students and time frame. For each session, we include three fun performance options: an exciting stunt, a fun improvisation and a traditional skit. Use as many or few as you want, and arrange them in whatever order best suits your VBS! For more information, see your copy of *Assemblies and Skits Production Guide*.

>> All our *Center Guides* feature an improved format for easier teacher preparation.

>> Service projects for every age level! See *Prekindergarten/Kindergarten Teacher's Guide* and *Theme Center Guide*.

>> The *Bible Story Center Guides* feature Old Testament Bible stories. For each lesson, we've included a New Testament Connection that ties to the Old Testament story and the focus of the session. This New Testament Connection shows how God's love and God's plans continue through the ages.

Expand Your VBS

Keep the spirit of VBS alive all summer long (or anytime!) with the curriculum designed to go along with SonForce Kids: *Agents in Action*, a 13-lesson adventure for children ages 3-12. The thrill of accomplishing daily missions for God as His special agents will challenge children to live courageously as His disciples. Use this course as a second-hour program on Sundays, a midweek evening program or any time you work with kids. You and your students will enjoy the flexible format and the variety of activities offered. *Agents in Action* is available from Gospel Light.

GOSPEL LIGHT'S 2007 VBS

SonForce Kids Course

SESSION	BIBLE STORY	FOCUS	BIBLE MEMORY VERSE	CRAFT
1 TRUST In God's Plans	Moses: Boy in a Basket Exodus 1—2:10	**PreK/Kindergarten** We can trust in God's love for us. **Elementary** We can have courage in all situations by trusting in God's love and plans for us.	**PreK/Kindergarten** "Trust in the Lord." (See Jeremiah 17:7.) **Elementary** "Blessed is the man who trusts in the Lord, whose confidence is in him." Jeremiah 17:7	**Early Childhood** Baby Moses in a Basket **Primary** SonForce Agent Badge **Middler** Moses Marble Maze **Preteen** Mission Patches
2 UNITE With God's People	Esther: Queen at Risk Esther 2—8	**PreK/Kindergarten** We can help others. **Elementary** We can have courage to stand up for others by uniting with God's people.	**PreK/Kindergarten** "With love, help each other." Galatians 5:13 **Elementary** "Be devoted to one another in brotherly love. Honor one another above yourselves." Romans 12:10	**Early Childhood** Jeweled Wristband **Primary** Palace Ornament **Middler** Courage Magnets **Preteen** Eye-See Can
3 TRAIN For God's Service	Daniel: Servant of God Daniel 1	**PreK/Kindergarten** We can do what is right. **Elementary** We can have courage to make wise choices by training to serve God.	**PreK/Kindergarten** "Listen to advice and you will be wise." (See Proverbs 19:20.) **Elementary** "Listen to advice and accept instruction, and in the end you will be wise." Proverbs 19:20	**Early Childhood** Veggie Concentration **Primary** Blast-Off Rocket **Middler** Create-a-Bot **Preteen** Wise Words Bookmark
4 FOLLOW In God's Path	Jeremiah: Prophet in Trouble Jeremiah 36—39	**PreK/Kindergarten** We can obey God, even when it is hard. **Elementary** We can have courage to follow in God's path, even when it is difficult.	**PreK/Kindergarten** "Obey me, and I will be your God." Jeremiah 7:23 **Elementary** "Obey me, and I will be your God and you will be my people. Walk in all the ways I command you, that it may go well with you." Jeremiah 7:23	**Early Childhood** Jeremiah's Scroll **Primary** Robo-Dog **Middler** Jeremiah's Message **Preteen** Spacewalk T-Shirt
5 LEAD Others to God's Promises	Joshua: Spy in a Strange Land Numbers 13—14:9	**PreK/Kindergarten** We can have courage because God promises to always be with us. **Elementary** We can have courage to lead others to God's promises.	**PreK/Kindergarten** "Be strong and courageous . . . for the Lord your God will be with you wherever you go." Joshua 1:9 **Elementary** "Be strong and courageous. Do not be terrified; do not be discouraged, for the Lord your God will be with you wherever you go." Joshua 1:9	**Early Childhood** Joshua and Caleb Take a Peek **Primary** SFA Promise Viewer **Middler** Pocket Computer **Preteen** Time Zone Gadget

GOSPEL LIGHT'S 2007 VBS

Overview   BIBLE THEME: JOSHUA 1:9

THEME CENTER	SONG	SNACK	RECREATION GAME	SKIT
Who Am I? Students experiment with different disguise techniques, decide on names and create identification badges as they prepare to be special agents. They learn that part of preparing as God's special agents is trusting Him and believing that His plans for our lives are the best. **Service Project Option:** Students make Surprise Packages by filling toilet-paper tubes with small gifts and short notes of friendship or encouragement.	"I Trust You with My Life"	**Moses in a Basket** Students place chow-mein-noodle baskets on graham crackers frosted with blue frosting to make a river. A jelly bean in the basket represents Moses.	**PreK/Kindergarten Jumpin' the River** Children jump over a pretend river. **Elementary Satellite Launch** Students play a game like volleyball using blankets to toss a foam ball.	**Mission Malfunction** Inez Halley and Jack Oort want to become Level 5 SonForce agents. They hope to impress Miss Newton with Robot's demonstration. But what is Edward Clark Felton doing with that remote control?
Create-a-Gadget Students use a variety of materials to make pretend gadgets that might be used to help others. They discuss how SonForce agents stand up for people who need help—even when it isn't easy—and that working together, or uniting, can give much-needed courage. **Service Project Option:** Students make Breakfast-in-a-Bag kits for homeless people.	"Together in Harmony"	**Queen Esther's Crown** Students use icing and candies to decorate crowns made from rice-cereal bars.	**PreK/Kindergarten Royal Races** Children wear crowns and run to touch a king's scepter. **Elementary Around the Galaxy** Players move a hula hoop around a circle by working together to pull hula hoop over and under each other without releasing hands.	**Asteroid Angst** An asteroid is on a collision course with Earth! But first, it threatens to smash into the SonForce Agency satellite station. Can special-agent partners Inez and Jack stop it? Or will they be stuck cleaning the bathrooms?
I Remember! Students play observation games as a training exercise. They discuss the importance of training to serve God and how it can give them courage to make wise choices. **Service Project Option:** Students decorate Home Service Envelopes and fill them with suggestions of services they can do at home.	"Train Me Up"	**Veggie Daniel** Students arrange vegetables into people shapes on paper plates, and then dip vegetables into dressing and enjoy!	**PreK/Kindergarten Vegetable Soup** Children use spoons to carry pretend vegetables and place them in a pot or box. **Elementary Special Agent Tag** Students play a game like tag to capture agents from the other team.	**Hero Worship** Miss Newton doesn't believe Inez and Jack when they reveal Felton is behind the asteroid threat! But now Felton realizes they're a threat to his plan to make himself a hero. What will Felton do to Inez and Jack?
Secret Writing Students experiment with different invisible-ink techniques and discuss how even though it is sometimes hard to follow in God's path, God promises to help us and give us courage when we need it. **Service Project Option:** Students make Thank-You Cards for people at VBS.	"Obey Me"	**Jeremiah's Scroll** Students make edible scrolls from fruit leather and pretzel rods.	**PreK/Kindergarten Pass the Scroll** Children play a game like Hot Potato with a scroll. **Elementary Avoid the Asteroid!** Students form spaceships and avoid being hit by asteroids (foam balls).	**Backdoor Breakthrough** The asteroid is minutes away from crashing into SonForce Agency! Inez and Jack know it's important to expose Felton as a fraud before anyone gets hurt. But what can they do tied up in a bathroom?
Send-a-Message Students try different fun ways to secretly send messages. Students discuss how we can become leaders by bringing God's messages to other people—helping them to know and believe God's promises. **Service Project Option:** Students make Follow-Up Envelopes to be mailed home to VBS visitors.	"Mission of Love"	**Promised Land Picnic** Students drizzle honey over crackers and enjoy snack with cheese and grapes.	**PreK/Kindergarten Falling Grapes** Children play a game with pretend grapes (balloons) and match colors. **Elementary Message Drops** Teams deliver balloon messages that review the Daily Missions.	**Remote Trouble** Oh, no! Felton thought he had everything under control, but now he can't stop the asteroid! Will Inez and Jack be able to stop it? Will Robot help? Will Felton realize what it really means to be a hero?

GOSPEL LIGHT'S 2007 VBS

Curriculum Ordering Guide

Select the Plan

Select the learning plan that works best for your VBS and list the SonForce Kids curriculum products that will meet your needs. This guide will help you calculate the number of materials you will need to order.

Activity Center Plan

Students travel in age-level groups, rotating from center to center throughout the day, escorted by Guides. (Modified Activity Center Plan assigns one or more teachers to each class for Bible teaching and life application, but students rotate through centers for all other activities.)

Plan:
Decide what centers you will offer, planning a maximum of 24 students in a center at a time. (Some large churches present the Bible story in larger groups and then complete Bible application in smaller groups. Some churches also lead recreation games, snacks and music in larger groups.)

Recruit:
You will need a teaching team for each center with one team member for every eight students (minimum of two team members for every center).

Order:
- *Director's Guide* and *Reproducible Resources* for the director
- Appropriate *Center Guide* for each team member
- *Teaching Resources* for each Bible Story, Theme and Bible Games center
- *Helper Handbook* for each Guide, helper or assistant
- *SFA Manual* for each student

Classroom- or Site-Based Plans

In the classroom-based plan, the teacher for each class teaches each day's Bible lesson and leads most or all of the other activities within a designated room. In the site-based plan, every day a teacher teaches the same entire lesson at the same location to a new class.

Plan:
Decide how many classrooms you will have, planning a maximum of 24 students in a classroom at a time.

Recruit:
You will need
- a teaching team for each classroom with one team member for every eight students (minimum of two team members for every classroom).
- Optional: Separate teams for crafts, music, snacks and/or recreation games. These teams either rotate to each classroom to lead activities or have a dedicated space to which groups rotate.

Order:
- *Director's Guide* and *Reproducible Resources* book for the director
- Appropriate age-level *Bible Story Center Guide* and *Teaching Resources* for each classroom
- *Theme Center Guide* and/or *Bible Games Center Guide* for each classroom
- *Special Agent Crafts for Kids* for each classroom or for craft team if done by a separate team
- *Songbook with Music Center Guide* and *SonForce Kids CD* for each classroom or for music team if done by a separate team
- *Recreation and Snack Center Guide* for each classroom or for games and snack leaders if done by a separate team
- *Helper Handbook* for each Guide, helper or assistant
- *SFA Manual* for each student

More Help Is Available

More help is available to you through www.myvbs.com (included in Super Starter Pack). In addition to providing your church with an instant VBS website, www.myvbs.com provides you with SonForce Kids clip art, an easy-to-use calendar, a budget calculator and additional helps for recruitment, training and publicizing your VBS. Visit www.myvbs.com to find out more.

Snapshot of SonForce Kids

Course Description

Invite your students to join SonForce Kids—God's courageous team of disciples standing side-by-side to serve Him. As SonForce special agents, they will follow in the words of Joshua 1:9: *Be strong and courageous. Do not be terrified; do not be discouraged, for the Lord your God will be with you wherever you go.*

The SonForce Kids headquarters is located on a satellite orbiting high above the earth. In this hi-tech command center, SonForce agents gather to prepare for their five Daily Missions: Trust! Unite! Train! Follow! Lead! Throughout VBS, your students will have the opportunity to grow in their understanding of what it means to serve God with courage as they advance from Level 1 to Level 5 agents.

From the courage shown by baby Moses' family, Level 1 agents will learn to **TRUST in God's Plans**. Following Esther's example, Level 2 agents will be encouraged to **UNITE with God's People**. To help them make wise choices like Daniel did, Level 3 agents will learn to **TRAIN for God's Service**. Just as Jeremiah obeyed God even when it was difficult, Level 4 agents will learn to **FOLLOW in God's Path**. Finally, like Joshua and Caleb, Level 5 agents will get ready to **LEAD Others to God's Promises**.

So get ready for an out-of-this-world adventure. SonForce Kids—courageous kids on a mission for God!

Set the Atmosphere

Add an unforgettable dimension to your VBS by filling your church with the sights and sounds of SonForce Kids.

Scenery

Use the patterns and ideas in *Reproducible Resources* and the "Decorating Ideas" segment of the *Preview DVD* to decorate your classrooms and activity centers. (Coloring Murals, Wall Cutouts, Star Disco Lights, Balloons, and Metallic Table Covers and Fringe Curtains are some of the decorating accessories available from Gospel Light.) Clip art is also available on our websites, www.gospellight.com and www.myvbs.com, and on the *Clip Art & Publicity CD-ROM*. Give your rooms or centers names appropriate for SonForce Kids: Mission Command (Assembly Room) for Opening and Closing Assemblies and Skits, The Pizza Pod for snacks, Tech Lab for crafts, Trans Port for Bible Story Center. Other centers could be called Outer Deck, Gadget Lab, Cyber Center, Robot Room, Welcome Station, etc.

Mission Command

Pizza Pod

Tech Lab

Trans Port

Sounds

The *SonForce Kids CD* provides lively songs to help your students learn Bible truths. These memorable songs help students and adults alike learn about God and His amazing love. See other suggestions under "Sound Off!" in "Bonus Theme Ideas" on page 11.

Fun Days

Enlist the help of VBS students and team members to set the stage for SonForce Kids VBS. Each day of VBS, ask students and team members to bring in or wear items to enhance the fun. Consider doing one or more of the following:

>> **Hat Day** Students and VBS team members wear fun, funny and fantastic hats that they bring from home or that they make at VBS using a variety of art supplies.

>> **Funny Hair Day** Encourage everyone involved in your VBS program to come up with his or her most outrageous hairstyle.

>> **Special-Agent Clothing** Ask students and VBS team members to wear sunglasses, dark jeans and SonForce Kids T-Shirts one day. On another day, ask everyone to come in disguise!

>> **Color of the Day** Using either the color of your choice or each day's Daily Mission Pennant as a guide, students and VBS team members wear the color of the day in their clothing or even their hair! Or have a Clash Day where everyone tries to make their clothing clash.

Staff Names and Group Names

Director of VBS Intelligence (DVBSI): Director

Special Agent in Charge (SAC): Activity Center Leaders, Guides

Supervisory Special Agents (SSAs): Adult and Youth Helpers

Group your students by

>> **Astronomical Objects:** Super Stars, Merry Moons, Plucky Planets, Quirky Quarks, Silly Satellites, Cool Comets, Great Galaxies, etc.

>> **Technological Objects:** Goofy Gadgets, Giggling Gizmos, Ready Robots, Computer Geeks, Cyber Cats, etc.

Bonus Theme Ideas

Use these extra-fun, theme-related ideas to create enthusiasm and excitement for your VBS.

Transitions

To signal transition times in your schedule, consider the following ideas:

>> Through your church sound system, play "SonForce Kids Theme" from *SonForce Kids CD*.

>> Blow an air horn.

>> Ask a volunteer to dress in a black suit and sunglasses or as VBS mascot (see p. 12) and walk throughout your campus, blowing a whistle or speaking through a megaphone.

Photographic Memories

In addition to or instead of the "Robo-Photo Stop" suggested on page 49, provide other photo opportunities at the Preview Event, the Closing Program or other special events. Other photo opportunities could include the following:

>> Students put on SonForce Kids T-Shirts and pose with skit actors dressed as their character (see *Assemblies and Skits Production Guide* for descriptions of skit characters).

>> In front of Mission Command or other backdrop, students wear black blazers and sunglasses and pose as if special agents, pretending to use headphones, cell phones, cameras, walkie-talkies, etc.

Use the photos as a way to follow up with unchurched families. After VBS, arrange for volunteers to hand-deliver the photos along with a church brochure that includes Sunday School and worship service times, as well as a description of different ministry groups and contact information. Include a prayer card which can be completed and mailed back to the church prayer team.

Mail Call

Teachers decorate cardboard boxes and place in classrooms. Prior to the first session, teachers write a short note for each student and place messages in the box. On the first day, teacher announces "mail call" and hands out messages to students. Students write messages to each other and place them in the box for the next session's mail call. Suggest students encourage each other to complete their Daily Mission: TRUST, UNITE, TRAIN, FOLLOW and LEAD.

Gift Shop

Near your welcome center and/or the place where parents pick up children, place a decorated table and several of the prizes and other fun items available from Gospel Light. Parents purchase items as presents for their children.

Sound Off!
Make your satellite station come to life using the sounds you might hear on a satellite station. During transitions between activity centers, have someone make announcements over a public-address system. Here are some suggestions: "Special Agent Gizmo: Please report to Cargo Bay 2. Your shipment of transponders has arrived." "All special agents scheduled to depart for Mission Mayhem on Mars: Your flight has been delayed. Please report to Shuttle Bay 8 at 2:00." The announcements could even be practical: "Level 3 Special Agents designated as Cyber Cats: You are to report immediately to the Tech Lab for craft training."

Acting Out
Another way to make your theme come to life is by staging mini-plays throughout your campus during transitions. As kids walk down the hallway, have some weird machine noises and taped conversation come from behind a closed door. As someone opens a door, fog from a fog machine fills the hallway. Ask skit actors and other volunteers who work behind the scenes to dress in costume (as robots and special agents—some in space gear!) and walk the halls discussing the "missions" they are working on.

Breaking News
In the weeks prior to VBS, place a colorful poster at the church door or in the lobby. Underneath, post VBS announcements: new staff additions, remaining vacancies, training meetings, etc.

Bandanna-Rama
With permanent markers and/or glitter pens, students print their names on neon-colored bandanas and add other decorations. Additional decorations might include Theme Buttons and Peel 'n Press Stickers (available from Gospel Light) or other art materials.

Let Me Hear It
Play songs from *SonForce Kids CD* through your hallways and outdoor areas.

Stickin' Badges
Each day of VBS, students complete another level of special-agent training. Recognize this achievement by giving each student a sticker badge to wear on their VBS T-shirts or name tags. "Agent Level Badges" are available as a sticker set from Gospel Light.

Satellite City
Provide a large variety of Lego building toys for students to use to create satellite stations. Kids build their own or work collaboratively to create one large satellite station. This activity can take place each day before VBS begins for kids who arrive early or after VBS has ended as kids wait to be picked up.

Guessing Game
In your gathering area or assembly room, prominently display a jar or bottle filled with a fun or theme-related item (marbles, small stars, rock or "asteroid bits," jelly beans, etc.). Kids guess the number of items in the jar or bottle to win prizes. (Bookmarks, Theme Buttons, Peel 'n Press Stickers, Skin Decals, Special Agent ID Tags, Blacklight Pens, Agent Sunglasses, Fold-Up Binoculars and Secret Message Scroll Pens are some of the theme-related prizes available from Gospel Light.)

Assembly Suggestions
Consider the following ideas to add fun and excitement to your opening and closing assemblies (for more information on assemblies, see *Assemblies and Skits Production Guide*):

>> Dress the part! Make sure your assembly leader wears theme-related clothing. A funny hat is always a crowd-pleaser. Consider purchasing or making hats shaped like a rocket, decorated with a fake mustache and glasses, with stars, etc. and wearing a different hat each day.

>> During your daily opening or closing assembly, toss out to assembled students or have a drawing for small prizes: plastic sunglasses, glow-in-the-dark necklaces, foam balls, other small toys or individually wrapped snacks. (Bookmarks, Theme Buttons, Peel 'n Press Stickers, Skin Decals, Special Agent ID Tags, Blacklight Pens, Agent Sunglasses, Fold-Up Binoculars and Secret Message Scroll Pens are some of the theme-related prizes available from Gospel Light.)

>> Every day have a puppet, or helper dressed as a skit character, a special agent character you have created, or your VBS mascot (see idea on p. 12) hide in the assembly room. Ask students to help you coax the puppet or character from hiding by whistling, calling out "Report for duty!" or using some other signal. After the first day, students will delight in discovering the puppet or character's hiding place. (Gadget Puppet available from Gospel Light.)

>> Have a daily trivia contest about the main person in each day's Bible story (Moses, Esther, Daniel, Jeremiah, Joshua). Have a leader, mascot, skit actor or other volunteer ask kids the daily trivia question(s) throughout the day at different activities. Kids who answer correctly receive small prizes and/or their names go into a container for a daily or weekly drawing for a larger prize. (Special Agent Voice Traps, Scramblers and Light Hands are available from Gospel Light.)

>> Use the "Countdown Sequence" from *The Asteroid Incident Skit DVD* as a way to get kids in their seats and ready for the assembly.

›› Ask a different VBS team member to give a brief, age-appropriate testimony during the closing assembly each day.

›› Make time for fun! Sing silly songs, play quick and easy games (Simon Says, I Spy, etc.), make a fool of yourself and simply enjoy your time with the VBS kids.

›› Arrange for a brief musical performance using a variety of instruments. Musicians can describe and/or tell interesting facts about the instruments and then perform songs.

›› Before VBS, have a weekend retreat for a group of 8-10 youth and/or adult helpers. During this weekend, volunteers learn the songs and motions, and rehearse the skits. When VBS begins, this group is ready and well rehearsed to perform skits during the opening assemblies and to lead songs during the opening and closing assemblies.

VBS Mascot

Consider a mascot who returns each year. Even if this mascot is an adult in an animal costume, he or she can dress in theme-related clothing and lead different segments of the assemblies, participate in various activities and interact with kids throughout VBS. Year after year, kids will look forward to the return of this character. For SonForce Kids, your mascot can wear dark glasses, a dark suit coat and tie.

Caught in the Act

Throughout the week, team members give prize tickets or toy money to children caught acting like a special agent serving God (sharing, caring, forgiving, etc.). Prize tickets or toy money may be exchanged for prizes.

Handy Passes

Using a rubber stamp and a stamp pad with black-light ink, stamp students hands every day as they arrive at SonForce Kids. Place a black light at each entrance to your assembly room. Students place their hands under the light to show that they have the stamp.

Snack Attack

Show your VBS staff that they are appreciated with a special lounge in which they can take their breaks, talk with each other, pray together and enjoy snacks prepared especially for them. Provide a variety of sweet and salty items along with beverages. Here are some suggestions that have proven to be popular:

›› **Brownie Bar** Provide brownies, ice cream, whipped cream, nuts, chocolate and strawberry syrup, candy sprinkles, cherries, etc.

›› **Ice Cream**
   ›› **Variety of Fresh Fruit**
   ›› **English-Muffin Pizzas**

›› **Chips and Dips** Serve a variety of chips, dips and salsas.

›› **Beverage Bar** Provide a variety of drinks: coffee, tea, iced tea, lemonade, bottled water, etc.

Autograph Day

Assign a day for volunteers and students to wear VBS T-shirts. Provide permanent markers for students, staff, skit actors and volunteers to use when signing each other's VBS T-shirts.

Guess Who

Each day post one or more pictures of someone from your VBS—staff or student. But instead of showing the whole picture, show only a portion: the eyes, arm, shoes, ear, back of the head, etc. Place a paper under the picture so that students can write down their guess as to who the person is. The first student to write a correct guess receives a prize. Or project the image during an assembly, and ask kids to shout out their guesses.

VBS Pins or Magnets

Put VBS stickers (available from Gospel Light) on poster board or craft foam, cut out and glue on pin backs or magnets. Use for prizes or have students arriving early at VBS make as a craft.

Add-On Prayer Journal

On a wall in the staff break room, display a large sheet of butcher paper. Draw a line down the center of the paper. At the top, print "Praises" on one side and "Requests" on the other side. Decorate with clip art (available on our websites, www.gospellight.com and www.myvbs.com, and on the *Clip Art & Publicity CD-ROM*). Keep pens nearby so staff can write praises and requests throughout VBS.

Prayer Rocket

Decorate a box with rocket images from *Reproducible Resources* or make box look like a rocket. Keep slips of paper and pencils next to box so that students can write down prayer requests and place in box. Each day, share requests at staff meeting and then refer requests to your VBS prayer team. If appropriate, include prayer requests during opening and/or closing assemblies.

Countdown

In your church bulletin and/or in the lobby of your church or other public area, provide a countdown beginning 10 weeks prior to your VBS: "Only 72 more days until SonForce Kids begins!" Each week update the countdown.

Dedication Service

Plan to hold a dedication service for VBS workers during a regular worship service. Enlist your pastor's approval and help. Print the names of volunteers in a bulletin insert and/or read names aloud. Volunteers come forward and stand while the pastor prays for them. Consider serving theme-related snacks after the service and/or provide special theme-related name tags for all the volunteers to wear. (Name Tag Holders available from Gospel Light.)

Get a Clue!
Each day of VBS, devise a secret message for your VBS special agents. (Because of varying skill levels, it is best to have a different message for each age level or class.) Beginning at the opening assembly and continuing at each activity throughout the day, students receive a clue to the secret message. The clue could be a riddle, scrambled word, puzzle pieces, etc. At the closing assembly, allow time for the classes to decipher the messages. Each class then tells the assembly the contents of their message.

Class Pictures
Select a different graphic image to represent each class (star, sunglasses, cell phone, rocket, etc.). Place die-cut (or photocopied and cut-out) images on sidewalks to form a path, leading from the welcome area to the place where the class gathers at the start of each day's VBS. Use the same image on name tags, class signs, bandanas, etc.

Daily News
Use the Staff Newsletters (see p. 55) to create a daily newsletter for your VBS team members. Customize the newsletters using the files available on the *Director's Guide CD-ROM* and your own word-processing application. Print important announcements, contact names and numbers, revised schedules or other changes, as well as anecdotes and/or photos from the previous day's activities. Pass out the newsletters at morning staff devotional time or place them in the staff break area.

The Golden Rocket
Make a rocket out of an empty potato-chip or oatmeal canister. Make triangles and a cone from fun foam or heavy card stock. Place lid on canister and glue cone over other end. Glue triangles at the bottom of canister to make fins. Spray paint gold. Use rocket in one or more of the following ways:

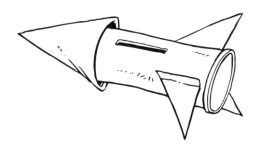

>> **Offering** If you collect an offering at your VBS, consider passing around the Golden Rocket to collect it. Cut a narrow slit in the side of the rocket for kids to insert coins and folded bills.

>> **Game** Hide the Golden Rocket on your church campus. At different locations throughout your campus, hide clues that will lead students from one clue to another, eventually discovering the hidden rocket.

>> **Award** Distribute Golden Rocket to a class at each session's Closing Assembly (see p. 59).

Visitor Recognition
Attach small prizes to helium-filled balloons and give one to each visitor and the student who brought him or her. Throughout the day, team members will be able to recognize visitors by the balloons and welcome them to VBS.

SonForce Kids on the Town
After VBS, dedicate a bulletin board or post a large sheet of butcher paper in a public area and ask kids to bring in pictures of themselves wearing their VBS T-shirts in various places: around town, on vacation, at school, etc. Keep it going year-round! With parent permission, the photos could be on a page of your church's website or in a newsletter. Send VBS T-shirts to the children of missionaries your church sponsors and ask them to send in their pictures, too!

Preview of Coming Attractions
On the last day of VBS, invite parents to come 20 minutes early to pick up their kids and treat them to a preview of upcoming special events and ongoing ministry programs for kids and families. Provide registration forms and ask your pastoral staff to be on hand to greet new families. Wrap up the assembly with a song, and tell families they can hear more great SonForce Kids music and learn all about what happened during VBS by attending the Closing Program. (See *Assemblies and Skits Production Guide* for more information about the Closing Program.)

Curriculum Resources
Familiarize yourself with the theme-related ideas provided throughout the curriculum. There may be ways to expand or adapt the ideas for use in other areas of your VBS. For instance, items made in the Craft Center can be used to decorate classrooms and hallways.

Panel of Experts
Visit the bulletin boards at the Gospel Light website, www.gospellight.com, for even more ideas shared by VBS directors from the United States and throughout the world!

GOSPEL LIGHT'S 2007 VBS

Materials Preview

Starter Kit

Your Starter Kit contains samples of materials that have been carefully designed to help you promote and conduct an effective SonForce Kids VBS. Each Starter Kit includes the following:

>> **Director's Guide**

>> **SFA Manuals** These colorful books for students are filled with Bible story reviews and fun, life-application activities. These guides are available for all age levels and are a tool teachers can use to make sure essential Bible truths are understood by students. Taken home, they help parents know what was learned and how to reinforce that learning.

>> **Bible Story Center Guides** These age-level teaching manuals contain what every leader needs to tell the Bible stories and lead life-application activities. In addition, the guides include reproducible teaching aids to make leading the Bible Story Center even easier.

>> **Teacher's Guide** This is a teaching manual for the early childhood teacher and contains all the information and reproducible helps needed to lead stories, activities, games and snacks for this self-contained classroom.

>> **Theme Center Guide** This teaching manual provides information needed to lead fun and exciting theme-related activities. Each activity includes a Service Project Option to help kids learn to serve God by helping others.

>> **Bible Games Center Guide** This teaching manual provides all the information needed to lead students in creative, theme-related games. For each session there are two games: one to review the Bible story and the other to review the memory verse.

>> **Recreation and Snack Center Guide** This is everything a leader needs to choose from a variety of theme-related games and snacks.

>> **Preview DVD** The "SonForce Kids Preview" on this DVD will give you a quick overview that you can use to introduce your VBS to your staff, congregation, etc. Also included on the DVD are decorating ideas, suggested motions for the SonForce Kids songs, missions information and recruiting commercials.

>> **Music CD Sampler** This CD features the SonForce Kids songs.

>> **Special Agent Crafts for Kids** This book contains 45 great craft ideas using readily available materials. There is a specific project in the craft book for every age and every session (see "SonForce Kids Course Overview," p. 6).

>> **T-Shirt** Fun-to-wear shirt that's the perfect souvenir.

>> **Director's Sample Pack** See description below.

Director's Sample Pack

This pack includes a sample of the following:

>> **Bookmark** Give away bookmarks as awards and prizes.

>> **God Helps Me Obey coloring book** This read-aloud story introduces children to the story of Daniel from Session 3.

>> **Evangelism and Discipling Booklets** *God Loves You!* and *Growing as God's Child* will help you talk with students about becoming members of God's family and learning to live as His children.

>> **Clip Art Sheet** Use this clip art for your newsletters, bulletins and other promotional materials. An attractive reproducible ad for use in your local newspaper or church newsletter is included. (Clip art is also available at www.gospellight.com, www.myvbs.com and on the *Clip Art & Publicity CD-ROM*.)

GOSPEL LIGHT'S 2007 VBS

>> **Peel 'n Press Stickers** These colorful stickers are perfect for awards and for charting students' progress and attendance.

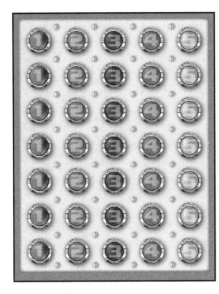

>> *Helper Handbook* This handy booklet helps train VBS staff and contains each day's devotional, Bible story, memory verse and lesson focus as well as a place for staff to record the essential information that they need.

>> **Coloring Contest Flyer** Invite children to VBS by distributing this fun-to-color reproducible poster at Sunday School, children's church, through the mail or in your neighborhood.

>> **Doorknob Hanger** Hang these colorful invitations to SonForce Kids on the houses near your church.

>> **Name Tag** Use these VBS name tags for each team member, student and visitor.

>> **Plastic Tote Bag** Give each student a perfect place to keep VBS papers and projects together. Provide one for each leader to store activity materials.

>> **Bulletin Cover/Insert or Promotional Flyer** These full-color 8½x11-inch (21.5 x 28-cm) sheets may be printed with your information on the back. Fold in half to use as bulletin covers, or cut apart to use as bulletin inserts or promotional flyers.

>> **Iron-On T-Shirt Transfer** Use this colorful design to identify VBS team members or to give every student a personal SonForce Kids memento.

>> **Student Certificate** These colorful certificates can be given to students for attendance and achievement.

>> **Volunteer Certificate** Recognize and thank the members of your VBS team with this certificate.

>> **Skin Decals** These colorful skin transfers feature the five Daily Missions.

>> **Theme Button** SonForce Kids buttons are a must-have for all your students and staff. Wear them for publicity, to generate enthusiasm and to remember the fun!

>> **Invitation Postcard** Mail these full-color postcards to prospective students. Instant e-postcards are also available at www.myvbs.com.

>> **Attendance Chart** This colorful chart coordinates with theme stickers. Use it to record students' attendance or Bible Memory Verse memorization.

>> **Photo Frame** These frames make great teacher thank-you items and are ideal for follow-up.

>> **Theme Posters** Advertise your VBS in the community with these beautiful posters. The Sample Pack includes both a large and small version of the poster.

>> **Special Agent ID Tags.**
>> **Secret Message Scroll Pen.**
>> **Agent Sunglasses.**
>> **Fold-Up Binoculars.**

Super Decorating & Resource Pack

This pack includes essential resources for activity leaders as well as exciting decorating helps.

>> **Teaching Resources** These colorful resources are filled with ideas and materials to enhance Bible learning. The *Prekindergarten/Kindergarten Teaching Resources* contains Bible story visual aids, Bible memory verse posters and theme-related posters. The *Elementary Teaching Resources* contains Bible Memory Verse posters, theme-related posters, Bible story posters and other teaching posters.

>> **Reproducible Resources** This book contains a wealth of decorating ideas and patterns, coloring pages, award certificates and more!

>> **SonForce Kids T-Shirt** These T-shirts are the perfect attire for VBS team members and students.

>> **Evangelism and Discipling Booklets** See description under Director's Sample Pack on page 14.

>> **Clip Art & Publicity CD-ROM** To build excitement about your upcoming VBS, use the clip art for your newsletters, bulletins and promotional materials. There are color as well as black and white images.

>> **Daily Mission Pennants** Use these colorful signs to designate classrooms, identify groups and review each session's Daily Mission.

Music & Skit Production Pack

In this pack you'll find everything you need to lead music, stage skits and present the Closing Program.

>> **SonForce Kids CD** This reproducible CD contains a split-track recording for performance of all the songs. Sound effects for skits and promotional radio spots are also included. Make copies of this CD for your students to take home or purchase the *Student Music Packs* described below.

Purchase CD Packs

Instead of duplicating the SonForce Kids music for all your VBS students and team members, you may purchase *Student Music Packs* of 10 CDs. These CDs contain all the SonForce Kids music.

>> **SonForce Kids Songbook** These songs make Scripture truths come alive for singers and listeners alike. The book contains songs and motions for all ages as well as Music Center activities for each session.

>> **Assemblies and Skits Production Guide** This reproducible book includes opening and closing assembly instructions, assembly performance options and skit scripts, a promotional skit, Bible story skits, tips for producing the puppet skits, instructions for the Closing Program and the Closing Program skit script. Also included are patterns and directions for making backdrops, props and set pieces. Use them to set the stage for your opening and closing assemblies as well as the Closing Program.

>> **The Asteroid Incident Skit DVD** Show the skits on this DVD as a rehearsal help for your live skits or during your VBS in place of live skit presentations.

Super Starter Pack

This pack provides all you'll need for the best VBS ever. The Super Starter Pack includes all of the items described above:

>> **Starter Kit** (including **Director's Sample Pack**)

>> **Super Decorating & Resource Pack**

>> **Music & Skit Production Pack**

With your purchase of the Super Starter Pack, you will receive a password to set up your own instant customizable website through www.myvbs.com. In addition, www.myvbs.com provides you with clip art, an easy-to-use calendar, a budget calculator and additional helps for recruiting, training and publicizing your VBS. Visit www.myvbs.com to find out more.

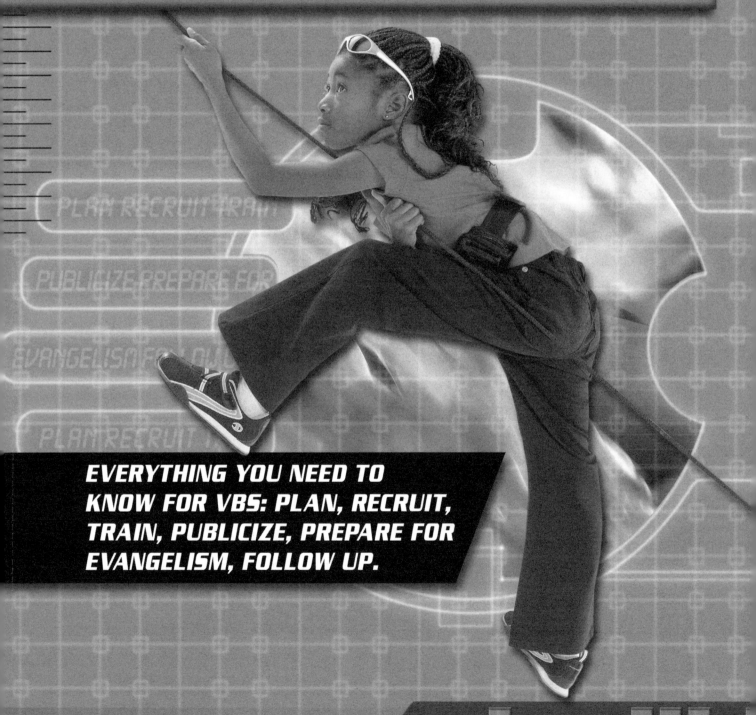

STEP-BY-STEP PLANNING GUIDE

EVERYTHING YOU NEED TO KNOW FOR VBS: PLAN, RECRUIT, TRAIN, PUBLICIZE, PREPARE FOR EVANGELISM, FOLLOW UP.

STEP-BY-STEP PLANNING GUIDE

1. PLAN

Summertime offers your church ideal opportunities for discipleship ministry and evangelistic outreach. Gospel Light's SonForce Kids is an effective and appealing VBS program that can help you reach students and families in your church and community. Every element of the course has been written with spiritual growth and teaching flexibility in mind. SonForce Kids can be used in a variety of formats.

Choose Your Format

Traditional 5-Day VBS

A 5-day program is still the most common choice for VBS. A morning or afternoon time slot works very well if your families have a stay-at-home parent. However, an evening VBS makes staff recruitment easier and avoids day-care conflicts. But be aware that an evening program will often need to be shorter and may limit the number of activities you can include in each session.

10-Day VBS

While the 5-day VBS program is easier to staff and operate, the 10-day VBS plan allows both learners and team members to explore more thoroughly the Bible stories, memory verses and life lessons. You can easily expand SonForce Kids into 10 days by using more of the activity centers and telling the Bible story one day and reviewing the same Bible story the following day. See specific expansion ideas in "How to Expand to a 10-Day VBS" on page 24.

Intergenerational VBS

This unique approach brings entire families together for parts—or even all—of the VBS activities. Instead of dropping their children off for VBS, parents stay and participate in activities specially designed to strengthen family relationships (see "Intergenerational VBS Guide," pp. 89-96).

Backyard Bible School

This format provides opportunities for neighborhood evangelism. Many children who do not attend church may feel more comfortable in the familiar surroundings of a neighbor's backyard than at a church (see "Backyard Bible School Guide," pp. 97-100).

Morning and Afternoon VBS

Some VBS directors face the problem of having more kids attending VBS than they have room for. What to do? Hold morning and afternoon sessions of VBS! Children of volunteers who work both sessions can attend VBS in the morning and participate in alternate activities (crafts, movies, field trips, etc.) in the afternoon.

Sunday-Morning VBS

Offer your VBS on Sunday mornings, from 9:00 a.m. to noon. While children are attending VBS, parents attend a worship service as well as a get-acquainted coffee time with a variety of special-interest presentations (child development, managing stress, discipline, etc.). Alternatively, offer an informal Bible study time. Our recommended adult Bible study for this adult class is *Wired That Way* (see VBS order blank).

STEP-BY-STEP PLANNING GUIDE

All-Summer VBS

You can hold your VBS on Saturdays throughout the summer. Use the 10-day plan and conduct one session each Saturday. This plan would also work for Wednesday night programs.

Camps and Retreats

You can use your VBS in a day camp, residential camp or weekend retreat format. For day camps, extend your VBS day by having students bring sack lunches and arranging field trips, movies, additional crafts and/or games for the afternoon. For camps or retreats, adapt your VBS materials as needed for an outdoor camp.

Choose Your Learning Plan

Once you've chosen your format, choose your learning plan. There are four basic learning plans from which to choose. Each plan impacts the tasks assigned to your staff and the daily schedule. (For information on who to recruit and what to order for each learning plan, see "Dear Director" on p. 5.)

Activity Center Plan

Individual activities are set up in specific locations. Outdoor areas, classrooms or large multipurpose rooms may be used for activity centers. Students travel in age-level groups, rotating from center to center throughout the day. Students are escorted by Guides, who may be adult leaders, adult helpers or youth helpers. Each center has one or two activity leaders who prepare and present only that specific activity as groups rotate through. This plan simplifies preparation for volunteers and allows them to work in their areas of strength, thus making recruiting easier (see "Activity Center Guide" on pp. 57-62).

Classroom-Based Plan

The leader for each class teaches each day's Bible lesson and leads most or all of the other activities within a designated room. This plan allows each classroom to be set up for a specific age group. This approach is recommended for early childhood classes, regardless of the plan chosen for older children.

Modified Activity Center Plan

Many churches prefer a modified approach in which a member of each group's teaching team teaches the Bible story in the Bible Story Center and then the team rotates with students through all other activity centers. This plan benefits from the advantages of the Activity Center Plan as well as providing an opportunity for the teaching team to bond with students.

Site-Based Plan

In this plan, every day a leader teaches the same entire lesson at the same location to a new class. For example, the first-grade class stays in one room and completes Session 5 activities on the first day of VBS. On the second day of VBS, the class moves to another room for Session 1 with a different leader. The main advantage is that leaders only need to prepare one lesson. Also, each room may be decorated for a particular Bible story.

There are several disadvantages with a site-based plan: First, activities that involve all the students, such as assemblies, cannot reinforce the Bible lesson for that day because each class has a different Bible lesson. Second, the lessons cannot progress chronologically or toward a climax because each class will be using a different lesson as the VBS concludes.

Prayer Team

Put the power of prayer to work for your VBS. Enlist a dedicated Prayer Leader (p. 28) to head up your year-round VBS prayer team. Volunteers meet regularly throughout the year to pray for VBS before, during and after VBS. Before VBS, volunteers pray about planning, recruiting and registration needs. During VBS, set up a special room where prayer can be ongoing throughout the day and visitors can join in. Use the Add-On Prayer Journal from the staff lounge (p. 12) to keep prayers focused on stated needs. After VBS, volunteers pray for VBS team members, students who attended VBS and those who made decisions for Christ during VBS.

© 2007 GOSPEL LIGHT. PERMISSION TO PHOTOCOPY GRANTED. SONFORCE KIDS *DIRECTOR'S GUIDE*

STEP-BY-STEP PLANNING GUIDE

Planning Your Early Childhood VBS

The Early Childhood Classroom

Young children have very specific physical and cognitive needs that differ significantly from those of school-aged children. As teachers we can best help young children learn Bible truths by providing active play experiences that are connected to Bible stories and verses through comments and questions.

This is why we recommend a classroom-based plan for early childhood classrooms, no matter which plan is used for elementary classes (see p. 19). In the classroom-based plan, children spend the entire session in the same classroom with a dedicated team of teachers. (Note: Separate craft and/or recreation leaders may lead those activities.) In addition to providing adequate time for learning, the self-contained classroom provides the sense of familiarity and security needed by young children.

> **Safety**
>
> Read "Special Safety Concerns for Early Childhood" on page 42.

Part of creating an environment conducive to learning for young children is having familiar items in the classroom. Some of these familiar items include:

- >> **Blocks** Wooden, plastic or cardboard blocks in different sizes, shapes and colors; toy people and animals; toy vehicles; manipulative building toys (Legos, Lincoln Logs, etc.).
- >> **Art** Crayons, markers and chalk; a variety of paper (construction, white, butcher, etc.); play dough and dough toys; child-sized scissors.
- >> **Dramatic Play** Dolls (with rubber molded heads), doll clothes and bedding; stuffed animals; home-living furniture (kitchen appliances, rocking chairs, doll beds, etc.) and accessories (dishes, toy food, dress-up clothes for both boys and girls, etc.). Include theme-related items such as items used for making disguises, toy cameras, toy cell phones, etc.
- >> **Books** Variety of picture books showing items and situations familiar to young children (nature, family, animals, friends, etc.). Include several theme-related books about special agents, stars and planets, space exploration, etc.

> **Note**
>
> Many churches find it helpful to recruit an Early Childhood Director (see p. 27) who oversees and trains early childhood teachers.

Schedule for Each Session

BEFORE CLASS

Teacher's Devotional

Every teacher should prayerfully read each session's devotional to prepare his or her mind and heart for this ministry.

Staff Prayer

Set aside a place where team members may come to pray before each session. Pray specifically for team members and students who have special needs. Allow a few moments for special announcements or last-minute organizational details.

CLASS TIME

Adjust the length of each time segment to best fit the needs of your VBS.

Bible Learning Activity Centers

(40-50 minutes)

Welcome Time At the door, a designated teacher welcomes and assists each child in choosing an activity center.

Activities Each teacher leads activity and conversation related to the Lesson Focus in one or more activity centers. Children are free to move from one center to another. Older children may rotate from activity to activity in groups. Don't worry if children don't want to participate in the suggested activity and instead create their own playtime activity. Teachers will still find the suggested conversation for each activity a helpful guide in talking about the day's focus.

Cleanup Time Teachers lead children in putting away materials.

Together Time

(10-20 minutes)

Teachers and children gather in one group for music, prayer, finger play, a puppet activity and Bible Words.

STEP-BY-STEP PLANNING GUIDE

Bible Story/Application
(15-20 minutes)
Children move to Bible story groups (about six children per teacher) or gather with entire class as one team member presents the Bible story using visual aids from *Prekindergarten/Kindergarten Teaching Resources*. Then team members sit at tables with children and guide them in completing Bible story and application activity pages from either the prekindergarten or kindergarten *SFA Manuals*.

Recreation Game/Snack
(20-40 minutes)
Team members (or a recreation leader) guide children in outdoor play activities and washup before snack. Check registration cards for any food allergies children may have. Also post a note each day alerting parents to the snack you will serve that day. Team members pray before snack, sit with children during snack and help as needed.

Skit
(10-15 minutes)
Each day for elementary students, a humorous skit is usually presented during the Opening Assembly or at another time. If prekindergarten and kindergarten children aren't included in the Opening Assembly, have skit characters visit your classroom to talk with children, or simply show a portion of *The Asteroid Incident Skit DVD*.

Craft
(15-20 minutes)
Children return to class groups or go to craft center to complete a project from *Special Agent Crafts for Kids*.

Music Fun/Good-Byes
(10-15 minutes)
Children gather for music, puppet time and indoor game activities until parents arrive. The inside cover of the *SFA Manual* is designed for children to place stickers for repeating the day's memory verse. Use SonForce Assortment stickers, available from Gospel Light.

Decorating the Early Childhood Classroom

Each day children will participate in one to four Bible Learning Activity centers in their classrooms. With a few decorations, each center can become a special place to visit at SonForce Kids. If you do not wish to set up all the centers, use or adapt any of the ideas to decorate your classroom. *Reproducible Resources* contains all the instructions and patterns you'll need for decorating. (Tip: Ask people who cannot otherwise help at VBS to assist in designing and decorating rooms before VBS begins.) The *Prekindergarten/Kindergarten Teaching Resources* includes a number of attractive posters to use in decorating the classroom and/or hallways. (Coloring Murals, Wall Cutouts, Star Disco Lights, Balloons, and Metallic Table Covers and Fringe Curtains are some of the decorating accessories available from Gospel Light.)

Early Childhood Classroom

STEP-BY-STEP PLANNING GUIDE

DIRECTOR'S CALENDAR

20 Weeks Before:

>> Pray, asking for God's help and guidance as you plan and organize your VBS.

>> Determine time, format, learning plan and location of VBS (Activity Center Plan, Backyard Bible School, camp, etc.).

>> Set VBS dates in conjunction with all-church calendar.

>> Order Starter Kit or Super Starter Pack.

18 Weeks Before:

>> Recruit an assistant director and publicity coordinator.

16 Weeks Before:

>> Meet with assistant director and publicity coordinator:
  1. Pray for VBS.
  2. Outline daily VBS time schedule.
  3. Set deadline dates for all preparations.
  4. List all staff needs.
  5. Compile lists of prospective workers.
  6. Plan training meetings.

>> Order curriculum materials for all center leaders, early childhood teachers and students (use last year's attendance reports as a guide).

>> Plan and order publicity materials.

>> Enclose a customized personnel recruitment flyer in the church bulletin or newsletter (see p. 30).

12 Weeks Before:

>> Begin personal contacts (letters and/or phone calls) to recruit rest of staff. In larger churches recruit department leaders and a craft leader for each age group.

10 Weeks Before:

>> Meet with leaders to plan training meetings and assign responsibilities.

>> Contact all recruits, confirming preliminary assignments and notifying them of training meetings.

>> Plan dedication service for workers (see "Bonus Theme Ideas" on page 10); secure minister's approval and help.

>> Meet with Special Events Coordinator and plan Preview Event and Closing Program.

>> Plan follow-up efforts with evangelism and Sunday School leaders.

>> Plan missions project.

8 Weeks Before:

>> Announce training meetings. Identify any new staff additions, remaining vacancies and plan additional recruiting efforts.

>> Make bulletin or newsletter insert listing needed craft supplies, refreshments and other materials.

This calendar is available as a full-size, color electronic file on the *Director's Guide* CD-ROM.

STEP-BY-STEP PLANNING GUIDE

4 Weeks Before:

>> Distribute curriculum samples to center leaders and early childhood teachers.

>> Conduct training meetings (see pp. 31-33).

>> Meet with the coordinators (missions, publicity, special events, finance, crafts, snacks, etc.) for prayer and to assess progress.

>> Begin preregistration, assign students to classes and prepare name tags.

>> Check donations and purchase additional supplies as needed.

>> Dedicate the VBS workers during church service.

During VBS:

>> Pray with and for your staff regularly.

>> Conduct morning staff devotions.

>> Distribute staff memos or newsletters.

>> Enthusiastically encourage workers with thank-you notes and daily visits to classes; make any necessary adjustments regarding staffing, transitions between activities, etc.

>> Make sure team members are present and on schedule and that attendance records are carefully kept and contact information is complete for each visiting student.

>> Assist with discipline problems and emergency situations as needed.

>> Distribute any announcements and flyers for children to take home on the appropriate days. Use the parent newsletters on the *Director's Guide CD-ROM* (see p. 56).

>> Secure additional supplies as needed.

>> Have someone available to run errands.

>> Be an "evangelism booster." Pray for and remind your staff to use the daily evangelism emphasis of SonForce Kids VBS.

>> Supervise the ongoing photography/videotaping of VBS activities.

>> Supervise preparations and build enthusiasm for the Closing Program. Send home Invitation Postcards to invite families to the Closing Program.

>> Present VBS awards and certificates to staff and children on the last day of VBS.

>> Distribute evaluation forms (What did you like best? What did you like least? What would you change? What was your greatest blessing?) Consider sponsoring a volunteer lunch at which team members complete and turn in forms.

>> Make sure all VBS volunteers clean up their areas on the last day of VBS.

After VBS:

>> Express appreciation to all workers with a note or a small gift.

>> Mail follow-up postcards to VBS visitors to begin contact efforts.

>> See that supplies are packed, labeled and stored for next year.

>> Compile all records, including sample flyers, bulletin announcements, newsletters, finance records and staff and student lists. Note how problems were solved and how to avoid similar problems. Include notes of necessary adjustments in schedules, additional supplies needed, etc.

STEP-BY-STEP PLANNING GUIDE

How to Expand to a 10-Day VBS
Elementary

SESSION	OPENING ASSEMBLY	SET THE STORY	BIBLE STORY	SFA MANUAL	ACTIVITY CENTERS
1	As written in *Assemblies and Skits Production Guide**	Option A: "Guess the Question" from each age-level's *Bible Story Center Guide*	Present Bible story as written in each age level's *Bible Story Center Guide*.	Review the Bible story by completing side one of each age level's *SFA Manual*.	Bible Games Center or Theme Center, Music Center, Recreation Game/Snack Center
2	Review songs learned previous day, ask questions to review skit or have preteen students perform skit*, review memory verse.	Option B: "Back It Up" from each age level's *Bible Story Center Guide*	Play "Phone It In" from *Bible Games Center Guide* or ask preteen students to perform skit from previous day's lesson to younger classes. (Bible story skits available in *Assemblies and Skits Production Guide*.)	Complete the life-application activity on side two of each age level's *SFA Manual*.	Craft Center, Music Center, Recreation Game/Snack Center
3	As written in *Assemblies and Skits Production Guide*	Option A: "Rocket Races" from each age level's *Bible Story Center Guide*	Present Bible story as written in each age level's *Bible Story Center Guide*.	Review the Bible story by completing side one of each age level's *SFA Manual*.	Bible Games Center or Theme Center, Music Center, Recreation Game/Snack Center
4	Review songs learned previous day, ask questions to review skit or have older students perform skit, review memory verse.	Option B: "Zig and Zag" from each age level's *Bible Story Center Guide*	Play "Disguise Pass" from *Bible Games Center Guide* or ask preteen students to perform skit from previous day's lesson to younger classes.	Complete the life-application activity on side two of each age level's *SFA Manual*.	Craft Center, Music Center, Recreation Game/Snack Center
5	As written in *Assemblies and Skits Production Guide*	Option A: "Agents in Training" from each age level's *Bible Story Center Guide*	Present Bible story as written in each age level's *Bible Story Center Guide*.	Review the Bible story by completing side one of each age level's *SFA Manual*.	Bible Games Center or Theme Center, Music Center, Recreation Game/Snack Center
6	Review songs learned previous day, ask questions to review skit or have older students perform skit, review memory verse.	Option B: "Tic-Tac-Toe Training" from each age level's *Bible Story Center Guide*	Play "Space Walk" from *Bible Games Center Guide* or ask preteen students to perform skit from previous day's lesson to younger classes.	Complete the life-application activity on side two of each age level's *SFA Manual*.	Craft Center, Music Center, Recreation Game/Snack Center
7	As written in *Assemblies and Skits Production Guide*	Option A: "Hoverboard Hustle" from each age level's *Bible Story Center Guide*	Present Bible story as written in each age level's *Bible Story Center Guide*.	Review the Bible story by completing side one of each age level's *SFA Manual*.	Bible Games Center or Theme Center, Music Center, Recreation Game/Snack Center
8	Review songs learned previous day, ask questions to review skit or have older students perform skit, review memory verse.	Option B: "Around and Around" from each age level's *Bible Story Center Guide*	Play "Back Me Up" from *Bible Games Center Guide* or ask preteen students to perform skit from previous day's lesson to younger classes.	Complete the life-application activity on side two of each age level's *SFA Manual*.	Craft Center, Music Center, Recreation Game/Snack Center
9	As written in *Assemblies and Skits Production Guide*	Option A: "Promise Plates" from each age level's *Bible Story Center Guide*	Present Bible story as written in each age level's *Bible Story Center Guide*.	Review the Bible story by completing side one of each age level's *SFA Manual*.	Bible Games Center or Theme Center, Music Center, Recreation Game/Snack Center
10	Review songs learned previous day, ask questions to review skit or have older students perform skit, review memory verse.	Option B: "Strip Slidin' Away" from each age level's *Bible Story Center Guide*	Play "Gear Up!" from *Bible Games Center Guide* or ask preteen students to perform skit from previous day's lesson to younger classes.	Complete the life-application activity on side two of each age level's *SFA Manual*.	Craft Center, Music Center, Recreation Game/Snack Center

* After skits are performed by rehearsed volunteers or the skit DVD is shown, preteen students who wish to participate in a live performance put their names into a drawing. Select performers for the next day's skit.

STEP-BY-STEP PLANNING GUIDE

Early Childhood

Repetition is wonderful for early childhood learners. So don't be afraid to repeat "Together Time" and "Music Fun/Good-Byes" as written, especially the games and songs. The familiarity of the activities on the second day will be reassuring to young children and will promote retention.

SESSION	BIBLE LEARNING ACTIVITIES	BIBLE STORY/ APPLICATION	RECREATION GAME/SNACK	CRAFT
1	"River Scenes" (Blocks), "Promise Cards" (Service)	Present Bible story as written. Complete Bible-story review activity on side one of appropriate age-level SFA Manual.	"Jumpin' the River" game; "Moses in a Basket" snack	"Baby Moses in a Basket" from Special Agent Crafts for Kids
2	"Caring for Baby" (Dramatic Play), "Play-Dough Kids" (Art)	Use Life of Jesus Poster to tell about Jesus. Complete life-application activities on side two of appropriate age-level SFA Manual.	"Hide the Basket" game; "Trail Mix" snack from Recreation and Snack Center Guide	"SonForce Gadget Belt" from Special Agent Crafts for Kids
3	"Esther's Palace" (Blocks), "VIP Crowns" (Service)	Present Bible story as written. Complete Bible-story review activity on side one of appropriate age-level SFA Manual.	"Royal Races" game; "Queen Esther's Crown" snack	"Jeweled Wristband" from Special Agent Crafts for Kids
4	"Let's Have A Party!" (Dramatic Play), "Helping Mural" (Art)	Use Life of Jesus Poster to tell about Jesus. Complete life-application activities on side two of appropriate age-level SFA Manual.	"Helper's Obstacle Course" game; "Milkshakes" snack from Recreation and Snack Center Guide	"My Own Computer" from Special Agent Crafts for Kids
5	"Table Builders" (Blocks), "Place Mats" (Service)	Use God Helps Me Obey big book to present Bible story. Complete Bible-story review activity on side one of appropriate age-level SFA Manual.	"Vegetable Soup" game; "Veggie Daniel" snack	"Veggie Concentration" from Special Agent Crafts for Kids
6	"Vegetable Gardens" (Dramatic Play), "Juice Painting" (Art)	Show God Helps Me Obey big book and let children tell Bible story events. Complete life-application activities on side two of appropriate age-level SFA Manual.	"Team Time" game; "Minipizzas" snack from Recreation and Snack Center Guide	"Band-Aid Bot" from Special Agent Crafts for Kids
7	"Block Builders" (Blocks), "Thank-You Cards" (Service)	Present Bible story as written. Complete Bible-story review activity on side one of appropriate age-level SFA Manual.	"Pass the Scroll" game; "Jeremiah's Scroll" snack	"Jeremiah's Scroll" from Special Agent Crafts for Kids
8	"Lovely Letters" (Dramatic Play), "Pretty Names" (Art)	Use Life of Jesus Poster to tell about Jesus. Complete life-application activities on side two of appropriate age-level SFA Manual.	"Let's All Follow" game; "Cookie Bags" snack from Recreation and Snack Center Guide	"Windsock Comet" from Special Agent Crafts for Kids
9	"Promised-Land Towns" (Blocks), "Give-Away Bags" (Service)	Present Bible story as written. Complete Bible-story review activity on side one of appropriate age-level SFA Manual.	"Falling Grapes" game; "Promised Land Picnic" snack	"Joshua and Caleb Take a Peek" from Special Agent Crafts for Kids
10	"Goin' on a Hike" (Dramatic Play), "Make a Map" (Art)	Use Life of Jesus Poster to tell about Jesus. Complete life-application activities on side two of appropriate age-level SFA Manual.	"Basket Balls" game; "Pudding" snack from Recreation and Snack Center Guide	"Disguise Kit" from Special Agent Crafts for Kids

STEP-BY-STEP PLANNING GUIDE

2. RECRUIT

Assessing Your Personnel Needs

One of the most valuable insights you will gain from directing SonForce Kids VBS is appreciating the impact it makes, not just on the children, but on the volunteers as well. VBS is an excellent opportunity for many people to find, use and develop their special gifts. Because it's a relatively short-term commitment and offers a variety of opportunities for service, even the easily intimidated can be a part of your VBS. The strong team spirit VBS creates carries over into the larger life of the church. Many who have never served before have found their beginning in VBS.

Begin the staffing process by assessing your needs. Read the staffing information in "Curriculum Ordering Guide" on page 8 and "Staffing Needs" beginning on page 27. Make a list of all the jobs that need to be done, no matter how small. Then determine which tasks can be combined to be done by one person.

Once you have identified the jobs to be done, factor in the team member-to-student ratio you want to maintain. The guidelines below will help you evaluate the number of volunteers you will need.

With your list of jobs in hand and the number of volunteers in mind, you are ready to take the next step.

Ratios

Team Member-Student Ratios

Early Childhood
For birth to two-year-olds:
1 adult for every 2 to 3 children.

For three- to five-year-olds:
1 adult for every 4 to 6 children.

Elementary
For six- to twelve-year-olds:
1 adult for every 6 to 8 children.

Important Note: For all age levels, there should always be more than one adult in the classroom at all times.

Guidelines for Success

Recruiting personnel is one of your most important duties as Director. You can build a strong VBS staff by keeping the following in mind:

>> Start early (see "Director's Calendar" on p. 22).

>> Pray for guidance in finding the right people to serve in this ministry.

>> Write a clear job description for each position to be filled (see "Staffing Needs" beginning on p. 27).

>> Build a list of prospective staff members including former VBS workers, youth, parents, college students and senior citizens (see below).

>> Share further recruiting responsibilities with the VBS leaders you recruit first.

>> Regularly present information to the congregation about your VBS program and volunteer opportunities. Show a segment of the "SonForce Kids Preview" or "Recruiting Commercial" from the *Preview DVD* in a church service. Distribute volunteer recruitment flyers in your church bulletin or in personal mailings.

>> Personally contact each prospect. Challenge each one with the importance of this ministry. Explain the training and resources you will offer to help the prospect succeed. If you must recruit a large number of people, schedule meetings with groups of prospects.

>> Allow the prospect time to pray about the opportunity. Resist the temptation to arm-twist; you don't want to end up with reluctant personnel.

>> Screen all potential staff. Use your church's forms and policies to select responsible volunteers.

Senior Citizens

Don't forget one of the great untapped resources in our society—senior citizens! These hard workers enjoy interacting with children of all ages and enjoy the freedom of retirement from work. Many churches find they serve well at the first day's welcome station—welcoming students and helping them find their classes.

Even those seniors whose health or schedule prohibit them from coming each day to VBS might enjoy being at-home workers. They can cut patterns, staple craft pieces, and otherwise prepare craft and other activity resources. Also consider asking them to fill out cards and certificates for students and staff.

STEP-BY-STEP PLANNING GUIDE

Staffing Needs

The following staff list includes a brief job description as well as suggested resources for each person in that position.

All VBS Plans

Director
Plans VBS format and schedule, recruits and trains staff and determines room assignments; oversees daily VBS activities.
>> *Director's Guide*
>> Director's Sample Pack
(Note: Both resources are included in the Starter Kit and the Super Starter Pack.)

Helpers
Team up with activity leaders to assist them with their responsibilities. These helpers can be adults or youth (see "Using Youth Helpers" on p. 29).
>> *Helper Handbook*

Secretary/Registrar
Plans and recruits staff to register children, maintain records and prepare visitor information for follow-up. May also perform duties of Follow-Up Coordinator.

Publicity Coordinator
Plans and carries out publicity to both church and community.
>> "Publicity Guide" (pp. 51-54)
>> *Helper Handbook*

Special Events Coordinator
Plans and recruits staff for closing program, field trips, promotional events and other special events.
>> "Special Events" (pp. 43-50)
>> *Helper Handbook*

Assembly Leader
Leads large-group assemblies (Opening Assembly, Closing Assembly, Closing Program). This job is often performed by the VBS Director or Skit Leader.
>> *Assemblies and Skits Production Guide*
>> *SonForce Kids CD*
>> *Helper Handbook*

Missions and Service Leader
Educates students and staff about chosen missions or service project; directs all missions or service project activities; collects and distributes donated money or other items.

>> "Missions and Service Center" (pp. 63-72)
>> *Helper Handbook*

Music Leader
Directs activities in the Music Center and leads or assists in leading singing during assemblies. Prepares children to present music during the closing program.
>> *SonForce Kids Songbook*
>> *SonForce Kids CD*
>> "Song Motions" from *Preview DVD*
>> *Helper Handbook*
>> Optional: Student Music Packs

Additional Staff Helpful for Directors of Larger Programs

Assistant Director
Helps Director with all responsibilities (in many churches this person will be next year's Director). Maintains daily time schedule.
>> *Director's Guide*

Decorating Coordinator
Plans and supervises decorating; recruits volunteers to help with decorating as needed.
>> "Decorating Ideas" from *Preview DVD*
>> Decorating section of *Reproducible Resources*

Early Childhood Director
Supervises departmental activities and helps recruit and train teachers and helpers.
>> "Early Childhood Planning Guide" (pp. 20-21)
>> *Teacher's Guide*

Nursery/Toddler Director
Supervises departmental activities and helps recruit and train teachers and helpers.
>> "Nursery and Toddler Guide" (pp. 73-86)

Elementary Department Leaders
Supervise departmental activities for primary, middler and preteen age levels. Helps recruit staff for each age level.
>> *Bible Story Center Guide* for the appropriate age level

Follow-Up Coordinator
Prepares and distributes correspondence from appropriate church contact people to unchurched VBS attendees. This role would be a natural fit for someone from your church's outreach/evangelism committee who understands children's ministry.
>> "Evangelism" (p. 35)

© 2007 GOSPEL LIGHT. PERMISSION TO PHOTOCOPY GRANTED. SONFORCE KIDS *DIRECTOR'S GUIDE*

STEP-BY-STEP PLANNING GUIDE

>> "Follow Up" (pp. 36-38)
>> *Helper Handbook*

Prayer Leader

Recruits people to pray for the team members, volunteers, students and families participating in your VBS.
>> *Helper Handbook*

Finance Coordinator

Plans budget and sees that money allocated for the program is spent appropriately.

Skit Leader

Auditions and/or recruits actors; schedules and directs rehearsals; supervises preparation of the backdrop and props.
>> *Assemblies and Skits Production Guide*
>> *The Asteroid Incident Skit DVD*
>> *SonForce Kids CD*
>> *Helper Handbook*

Youth Coordinator

Enlists, trains and supervises middle school and high school youth serving as helpers in VBS.
>> "Using Youth Helpers" (p. 29)
>> *Helper Handbook*

Activity Center Plan

Recruit a teaching team—one team member for every six to eight students—for each of the activity centers you have chosen for your VBS. Remember, there should be at least two adults in each classroom at all times.

(Note: We recommend the classroom-based model for early childhood classes. See "Classroom-Based Plan" on p. 19 for the resources needed by these leaders.)

Guides

Essential to the Activity Center Plan are the Guides. Each adult Guide escorts a group of students to the different activity centers. Because they spend the entire session with one group of students, the Guides are able to build relationships with children, assist with various activities and maintain discipline. Guides should be prepared to talk and pray with students about becoming members of God's family. (Note: Some churches combine the positions of Guide and Bible Story Leader.)
>> *Helper Handbook*
>> *God Loves You!* and *Growing as God's Child* booklets

Elementary Bible Story Leader

Teaches the Bible story and leads the life-application time as each group of students visits the Bible Story Center. (Note: Some churches combine the positions of Guide and Bible Story Leader.)
>> *Bible Story Center Guide* for each age level
>> *Elementary Teaching Resources*
>> *SFA Manuals*, one for each student

Craft Leader

Chooses craft projects, gathers materials, explains and supervises the crafts as each group of students visits the Craft Center; may recruit helpers.
>> *Special Agent Crafts for Kids*
>> *Helper Handbook*

Recreation Game Leader

Chooses games, gathers supplies and leads students in playing the games; may recruit helpers.
>> *Recreation and Snack Center Guide*

Snack Leader

Chooses snacks, gathers ingredients, recruits helpers and leads groups of students in the preparation of daily snacks.
>> *Recreation and Snack Center Guide*

Bible Games Leader

Plans, gathers materials and leads games as each group of students visits the Bible Games Center. Uses suggested conversation to help students review each day's Bible story and/or Bible memory verse and apply them to their lives.
>> *Bible Games Center Guide*
>> *Elementary Teaching Resources*

Theme Center Leader

Plans, gathers materials and leads activities as each group of students visits the Theme Center. Uses suggested conversation to link students' activities to their everyday lives.
>> *Theme Center Guide*
>> *Elementary Teaching Resources*
>> *Helper Handbook*

Classroom-Based, Site-Based and Early Childhood Plan

Decide how many classrooms you will have, planning a maximum of 24 children in a classroom at one time. Recruit a teaching team—one team member for every four to six children—for each classroom. Remember, there should be at least two adults in each classroom at all times.

Age-Level Teachers

Plan and present the entire lesson (Bible story, games, music, crafts, etc.) to a class in one classroom.

For Each Elementary Teacher:

>> *Bible Story Center Guide* for appropriate age level
>> *Bible Games Center Guide*
>> *Theme Center Guide*
>> *SFA Manuals* for appropriate age level, one for each student
>> *Elementary Teaching Resources*
>> *Special Agent Crafts for Kids*

If teacher is also teaching music, he or she will need

>> *SonForce Kids Songbook and DVD*
>> *SonForce Kids CD*

For Each Early Childhood Teacher:

>> *Teacher's Guide*
>> *SFA Manuals* for appropriate age level, one for each student
>> *Prekindergarten/Kindergarten Teaching Resources*
>> *Special Agent Crafts for Kids*

If teacher is also teaching music, he or she will need

>> *SonForce Kids Songbook and DVD*
>> *SonForce Kids CD*

Using Youth Helpers

Many churches find great value in using middle school and high school youth in leadership roles at Vacation Bible School. It's good for the children—they readily admire and enjoy following a young person's guidance and look forward to becoming helpers themselves. It's good for the adult staff—they benefit from the energy and enthusiasm of young assistants. And it's good for the young people—they gain valuable ministry experience and personal spiritual growth.

The guidelines below have proven helpful to others.

>> Far in advance of VBS, **talk with the church's youth leaders** about involving young people. Enlist their support in encouraging youth participation. Seek to involve at least some of the youth leaders in various phases of VBS and its preparation.
>> Recruit a **Youth Coordinator** (see description under "Staffing Needs," p. 28).
>> Define **requirements** for the young people. Within the framework of your church's youth programs and child-safety policies, set standards that will challenge young people while being as inclusive as possible. Often youth will blossom when given the opportunity to serve. Consider developing a contract to use with your youth. The contract could outline time commitments and responsibilities of youth helpers. Make sure both the youth and their parents sign the contract.
>> Decide on the **positions** young people can fill. The specific tasks may vary depending on how you structure your VBS.

All VBS Plans:

1. Skit performers, musicians, Bible verse listeners and other positions specific to your VBS.

Activity Center Plan:

1. Youth helpers assist adult Guides and stay with the same group of students as they move from activity to activity, focusing on building friendships and keeping students involved. It is a good idea to have both a boy and a girl with each group of students, providing role models for both genders.
2. Youth helpers stay in an assigned activity area (Bible story, crafts, games, snack, etc.), assisting the leader(s) with specific functions.

Classroom-Based and Early Childhood Plan:

1. Youth helpers assist leaders and stay in the same room with the same children and staff for most activities, performing a combination of tasks.

>> **Enlist** young people to serve. At least several months in advance of VBS, begin announcing this opportunity to youths and their parents. Provide recruiting flyers to interested youths (see p. 30). Promote the benefit of including youth helpers to your congregation and VBS families. Present it as a great opportunity for children to benefit from positive youth role models.
>> Working with your Youth Coordinator, prayerfully **assign** specific positions to your youth helpers.
>> Schedule one or more **training sessions** in advance of VBS just for the youth helpers. Make the sessions very specific in covering what you expect of them. Provide each volunteer with a copy of the *Helper Handbook* and go over its material during your training session(s). It is important that youth helpers be familiar with each day's focus, Bible memory verse and Bible story. Challenge them to make this event more than just a fun time playing with the children.
>> **Prepare** your adult staff to work with the youth helpers. Provide the adults with information explaining the youth helpers' responsibilities.

STEP-BY-STEP PLANNING GUIDE

Encourage adults not to limit young people to busy work, but to also assign jobs the young person will view as meaningful.

>> Schedule at least one **meeting** with all staff together to help adults and youth get to know each other and to finalize plans and assignments for each person.

>> During VBS, plan for ways to make sure youth helpers have a **good time** and feel appreciated. Ideas to accomplish this:

1. Provide a special treat each day.
2. Encourage the children to thank their youth helpers. (Affirmation from children is one of the biggest benefits helpers will receive.)
3. During each opening or closing assembly, comment on the great job the youth are doing.
4. Have a youth leader, one who already knows the youth, make a point of checking in with each young person, affirming their work and seeing if there are any problems or difficulties.
5. Schedule a special event just for the youth helpers, such as a pizza party, a picnic in the afternoon, a social event in the evening, etc.

After VBS, your youth helpers will be trained to go even further in ministry. Pack up your decorations and leftover materials and send them on the road with your youth helpers! Teams of teens can bring VBS to communities where kids wouldn't normally get a chance to attend VBS. Your youth will gain precious ministry experience as they bless these kids and their communities.

Sample Flyers for Staff Recruitment

These samples are available as full-size, color electronic files on the *Director's Guide CD-ROM*.

Vacation Bible School Volunteers

Dates _____ Time _____

I would like to help in one or more of the following areas (please circle):

- Decorating
- Publicity
- Bible teaching
- Group Guide
- Music
- Snacks
- Follow-up
- Prayer support
- Missions project
- Crafts
- Recreation games
- Skits
- Special events
- Youth helper
- Other _____

Name _____
Address _____
Phone (day) _____
Phone (evening) _____
E-mail _____

If you have any questions about Vacation Bible School or your involvement in it, please call

_____ (name and phone number)

PLEASE RETURN THIS FLYER IN THE OFFERING PLATE OR TO THE CHURCH OFFICE.

Vacation Bible School Volunteers

Dates _____ Time _____

Before VBS, I would like to help by (circle one or more):

- Praying for team members and children
- Providing craft materials
- Preparing craft materials
- Planning decorations
- Decorating
- Gathering props for decorations and/or skits
- Planning publicity
- Distributing publicity materials
- Painting banners, backdrops, sets, etc.
- Preregistering children
- Planning special events (promotional day, field trips, etc.)
- Assisting with special events
- Contacting local businesses to donate food and other items for VBS

During VBS, I would like to help in one or more of the following areas (please circle):

- Bible Story Center — Leader / Helper
- Bible Games Center — Leader / Helper
- Theme Center — Leader / Helper
- Craft Center — Leader / Helper
- Recreation Game Center — Leader / Helper
- Snack Center — Leader / Helper
- Music Center — Leader / Helper
- Missions — Leader / Helper
- Special Events — Leader / Helper
- Secretary/Registrar
- Skit Director
- Actor
- Photographer/Videographer
- Assembly Leader
- Follow-Up
- Helper

Age-Level Preference

- Nursery and Toddler
- Prekindergarten (3-4 yrs.)
- Kindergarten (5 yrs.)
- 1st grade
- 2nd grade
- 3rd grade
- 4th grade
- 5th grade
- 6th grade

Name _____
Address _____
Phone (day) _____ Phone (evening) _____
E-mail _____

If you have any questions about Vacation Bible School or your involvement in it, please call

_____ (name and phone number)

PLEASE RETURN THIS FLYER TO THE CHURCH OFFICE.

3. TRAIN VOLUNTEERS

There are basically two types of training sessions that should be conducted: general (for all staff) and specific (age-level or leadership staff).

A **general meeting** for all volunteers is absolutely necessary for communicating basic VBS information. One or two meetings are all that you will probably need to have. These meetings should include the following:

>> Introduction to the curriculum (theme, lesson focus, theme verse, etc.)

>> Pertinent general information (dates, time schedule, locations, supplies, future meetings, etc.)

>> Opportunity to fellowship

Specific meetings should then be conducted by the Director or by age-level leaders. The nature of these meetings depends on the needs of the staff. Topics that may be covered in these sessions:

>> Planning and preparing lessons

>> Decorating and preparing your classroom

>> Use of the curriculum

>> Age-level characteristics

>> Leading children to Christ (see individual *Center Guides* or the inside back cover of *Helper Handbook*)

>> Dealing with discipline

>> Building relationships

>> Storytelling techniques

>> Following up after VBS

Preparing for the Meetings

>> Schedule each meeting at a time you think most volunteers will be able to attend. Many churches schedule their meetings on Saturday morning or Sunday after church. Provide child care if needed. Reserve your chosen dates on the church calendar.

>> As you begin recruiting, make sure you let all volunteers know the dates of your meetings—either in person, by phone, by mail or by e-mail. Publicize each meeting in your church bulletin. Then mail reminder notices at least five days in advance. Make your notices look attractive and exciting, and be sure to include the date, time and place. Follow up with personal phone calls.

>> Plan each meeting's agenda. Write down all the information and topics you wish to cover. Have specific goals, and plan specific steps to meet them. If other individuals will lead parts of the meeting, make sure you give them plenty of advance notice. Begin brainstorming ideas on how to add excitement and variety to your presentation. Consider using visuals, music, games, videos, etc.

>> Make a list of all the supplies you will need for each meeting. Secure important curriculum items such as the *Preview DVD, The Asteroid Incident Skit DVD, SonForce Kids CD*, posters, *Center Guides* and any other helpful promotional items. Also make sure you have tables, chairs, CD player, a television, DVD player and overhead projector, if needed.

>> Plan to serve refreshments. Refreshments show your volunteers you appreciate their attendance. The food can be as simple as coffee, iced tea and cookies or can be expanded to include theme-oriented snacks. (See *Recreation and Snack Center Guide*.)

>> Personalize each meeting. Purchase or make name tags for all your volunteers—don't assume everyone knows each other. (Name Tag Holders available from Gospel Light.) Provide a sign-in sheet to give your volunteers a sense of accountability. Purchase little treats such as candy, VBS buttons or pins, note pads and/or tote bags for each participant.

STEP-BY-STEP PLANNING GUIDE

Sample General Training Meeting

The following is an example of a general staff training meeting. Adapt it to fit your particular needs.

Before the Meeting

>> Display any promotional posters, banners or other promotional items from the curriculum.

>> Place chairs in semicircles around tables so that they face one wall.

>> Arrange to have a CD player, a television and a DVD player.

>> Liven up the room with some theme-oriented decorations.

>> Place a sign-in sheet, name tags and pencils on a table.

>> Set up a refreshment table.

>> Place handouts and a simple treat on each seat.

During the Meeting

>> While volunteers arrive and gather, play music from *SonForce Kids CD* in the background.

>> Greet each person at the door and invite each one to sign in, make a name tag and enjoy the refreshments. Ask them to think of a special-agent name to add to their name tag.

>> After volunteers are seated, enthusiastically welcome the group and open with prayer. Express appreciation for their attendance and assure them that this meeting will be worth their efforts.

>> Give a brief overview of SonForce Kids using the Course Overview (pp. 6-7) and Course Description (p. 9).

>> Show the "SonForce Kids Preview" from the *Preview DVD*.

>> Introduce the VBS committee and each of the coordinators/directors. Ask these leaders to share in a few words their duties, with whom they will be working and any goals they might have.

>> Using the inside front cover of the *Helper Handbook* or a form you've prepared, have helpers write down important contact information, review the daily schedule (including staff devotions), note their room assignments, detail emergency procedures and record other important information.

>> Have your Publicity Coordinator share ideas and events for promoting SonForce Kids. Explain how all the volunteers can participate in promotion.

>> Have your Music Center Leader teach and demonstrate the motions to "God's Kids," "Be Strong and Courageous" or another SonForce Kids song. Also have the Music Center Leader or Special Events Coordinator share the date, time and events planned for the Closing Program.

>> Explain your procedure for securing and/or purchasing supplies. Distribute pertinent forms.

>> Have age-level leaders distribute any curriculum items or other important materials to their teams.

>> Allow teams about 15 minutes to meet with each other to review their job descriptions and deadlines and to schedule additional meetings.

>> Bring groups together. Give individuals a chance to ask any general questions.

>> Close in prayer and dismiss.

After the Meeting

>> List all items that require follow-up, with dates to be done and person(s) responsible for the task. Check off each item as it is accomplished.

>> Write a short summary of the meeting, noting topics discussed, decisions made, etc. Include your evaluation of the meeting's success and thoughts on how to improve for the next one. Refer to this evaluation in planning for your next meeting.

Sample Age-Level Training Meeting

Schedule, or ask age-level leaders to schedule, a planning meeting for team members several weeks before VBS.

Before the Meeting

>> Carefully read the information provided about learning aims, activity centers and schedule.

>> Give each team member the resources listed in "Staffing Needs" (see p. 27). Ask them to read "Age-Level Characteristics" in their guides or handbooks.

>> Assign volunteers to prepare different

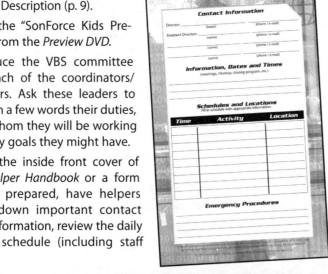

STEP-BY-STEP PLANNING GUIDE

elements of the lesson for Session 1 and to be able to explain how each helps meet the lesson aims.
For early childhood: Bible story and visuals, *SFA Manual*, Bible Learning Activities, craft, game, snack, songs, use of puppet, finger play, etc.
For elementary: Bible story and appropriate involvement options, *SFA Manual*, Bible Games Center game(s), Theme Center activity, craft, recreation game, snack, songs, etc.

>> Ask the Assembly Leader, Skit Leader, an actor or other volunteer to preview the skit and be able to describe how the skit reinforces the lesson aims.

>> Gather and set up all necessary supplies and equipment: overhead projector and screen, television and DVD player, CD player, pens, paper, etc.

>> Arrange the room for the comfort and ease of volunteers. Make sure they can see and reach everything they need.

>> Have sufficient copies of all handouts ready to pass out.

During the Meeting

>> Begin on time. Pray together and ask God to help you express His love to children in ways they can understand.

>> Briefly review the following items, answering questions as needed:
 1. Each session's learning aims;
 2. The daily schedule;
 3. The responsibilities of each leader and helper. For early childhood classes, decide which Bible Learning Activity centers to offer each day, with each leader selecting an activity to lead. Make special assignments such as greeting children, recreation responsibilities and snack preparation.

>> Walk through Session 1 by having volunteers share prepared assignments.

>> Make any special assignments for the week. Discuss each age-level's role in the Closing Program.

>> Make plans for follow-up of children and discuss additional ideas for reaching unchurched families.

>> Answer any questions. Dismiss in prayer.

After the Meeting

>> List all the items that require follow-up, with dates to be done and person(s) responsible for the task. Check off each item as it is accomplished.

>> Write a short summary of the meeting, noting topics discussed, decisions made, etc. Include your evaluation of the meeting's success and thoughts on how to improve if there is need for another one. Refer to this evaluation in planning for any additional meetings.

Hints for Successful Meetings

>> Arrive early. Having everything planned and set up in advance provides a positive example for your volunteers. You can't expect your volunteers to do more than you're willing to do yourself.

>> Use the SonForce Kids theme to build excitement. Reinforce the theme through the use of music, decorations, clothing, refreshments, prizes, etc. (Bookmarks, Theme Buttons, Peel 'n Press Stickers, Skin Decals, Special Agent ID Tags, Blacklight Pens, Fold-Up Binoculars and Secret Message Scroll Pens are some of the theme-related prizes available from Gospel Light.)

>> Provide some time for fellowship. Start each meeting with an icebreaker game or other fun event. This will help your volunteers become familiar with one another, build friendships and foster team unity.

 One icebreaker suggestion would be to ask everyone to answer the question, "If you were a special agent, what gadget would you most want to have and why?"

>> Make the meetings worthwhile. Though fun can be on the agenda, volunteers should not feel that they have wasted their time. Make sure all information is clearly presented.

>> Start and end meetings on time. This shows your volunteers that you respect their schedules. Allow about five minutes for volunteers to arrive before beginning the meeting.

STEP-BY-STEP PLANNING GUIDE

4. PUBLICIZE

Below is a list of ways to promote SonForce Kids VBS within both your church and your community. For an explanation of how to use each item listed, a suggested publicity calendar and other helps, see "Publicity Guide" on pages 51-54 and "Preview Event" on pages 45-50.

Build VBS Interest Within the Church

>> Bulletin Insert
>> *Preview DVD*
>> VBS Video/Slideshow
>> Posters
>> Sunday School Visits
>> Church Website
>> Information Booth
>> VBS Buttons and T-Shirts
>> SonForce Kids Skits
>> Music

Reach Out to Children from the Community

>> Outdoor Banner or Sign
>> Posters
>> Invitation Postcards
>> Promotional Flyers and/or Doorknob Hangers
>> SonForce Kids Skits
>> Radio
>> Newspaper, Television and Other Media
>> Preview Event
>> Preregistration Bonuses
>> Direct Mail
>> Prizes
>> Parents' Class

SonForce Kids Registration, VBS 2007

This form is available as a full-size, color electronic file on the *Director's Guide CD-ROM*.

SonForce Kids Registration, VBS 2007

Name _____
Birth date _____ School grade just completed _____
Street address _____
City _____ State _____ Zip _____
Home phone (____) _____ Cell phone (____) _____
E-mail _____
Parent(s) name(s) _____
Parent(s) work phone(s) _____
   In case of emergency, contact _____
   Allergies or other medical conditions _____
   Name of home church, if any _____

STEP-BY-STEP PLANNING GUIDE

5. PREPARE FOR EVANGELISM

The apostle Paul wrote, "I pray that you may be active in sharing your faith" (Philemon 1:6). SonForce Kids presents a unique opportunity to share the gospel and win people to Christ.

Give team members the Gospel Light booklets *God Loves You!* (for leading children to Christ) and *Growing as God's Child* (for follow-up and discipling).

Ask team members to read the article "Leading a Child to Christ" available in each *Center Guide*, *Teacher's Guide* and *Helper Handbook*.

Be sure team members are familiar with the lessons in the *Bible Story Center Guides*. Each lesson provides an opportunity for evangelism as part of the Conclusion (look for the evangelism opportunity symbol).

Instruct team members to invite responses by saying, "If you're interested in knowing about becoming a member of God's family, I'll be here after class to talk with you." Children sometimes feel hesitant to seek out busy adults, so encourage team members to be ready to schedule a brief quiet time to talk informally with individual children.

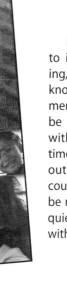

© 2007 GOSPEL LIGHT. PERMISSION TO PHOTOCOPY GRANTED. SONFORCE KIDS *DIRECTOR'S GUIDE*

STEP-BY-STEP PLANNING GUIDE

6. FOLLOW UP

Follow Up on Children and Families

>> Before VBS begins, have the Follow-Up Coordinator prepare various notes to be mailed to each visiting student and family after VBS. Notes may be sent from the VBS Guides or leaders, the pastor and/or a potential Sunday School teacher. Names and addresses can be obtained from the Secretary/Registrar. Have team members personalize and sign these notes during VBS. The Follow-Up Coordinator can mail them in the week or two following VBS.

>> During VBS the Follow-Up Coordinator should distribute daily newsletters with each student (see pp. 27-28). These newsletters thank parents for sending the student, inform parents what kids are learning each day at VBS, invite families to attend the Closing Program, offer a visit from a church leader and provide a way to suggest other family-oriented programs that your church provides. Use the newsletter files available on the *Director's Guide CD-ROM* (see pp. 55-56).

>> Suggest that Sunday School teachers attend the Closing Program. Ask age-level Guides to introduce visiting children and their parents to the appropriate Sunday School teachers.

>> At the Closing Program, set up a free family photo opportunity with simple costumes and a backdrop. (For suggested photo opportunities, see "Photographic Memories" in "Bonus Theme Ideas" section beginning on p. 10.) After photographs are printed, place in a fun frame (theme-related Photo Frame available from Gospel Light) and arrange for volunteers to deliver them to unchurched families along with a brochure describing your church's ministry programs. If home visits are not possible, have parents address envelopes when photos are taken. Mail photos, brochures and a personal note in the week following VBS.

>> If you present a video or slideshow of VBS highlights during your Closing Program, offer to give copies to families. After VBS, have volunteers make and distribute videocassettes or CDs along with a church-ministry brochure.

>> Present a participation certificate to each student and an appreciation certificate to each volunteer. Samples of full-color certificates are available in the Director's Sample Pack and can be ordered in bulk from Gospel Light. Reproducible certificates are available in *Reproducible Resources*.

>> Create a mailing list of all unchurched families from VBS. Give the ministry leaders within your church a copy of the mailing list to send promotions about other church events.

>> Recruit volunteers to call children and their families in the weeks following VBS to tell them of upcoming church events and inquire if they have any questions about the church and its ministry programs.

>> Ask church families to invite unchurched families to Sunday School and church. Church families can offer to provide transportation, meet visitors at the door, sit with them and introduce them to others.

>> Plan a children's or family activity in the month following VBS (see "Special Events," pp. 43-50). Distrib-

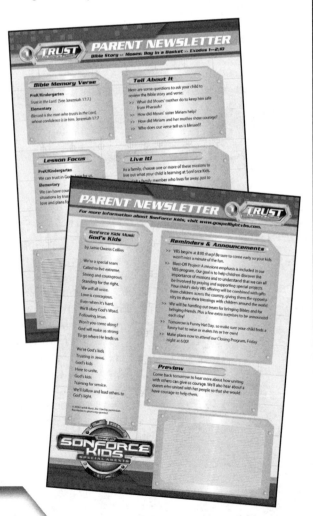

STEP-BY-STEP PLANNING GUIDE

ute a flyer during VBS and mail a flyer to each new visitor a week or two prior to the event. Finally, give each visitor's family a friendly invitation by phone the week leading up to the event.

>> Keep the spirit of VBS alive all summer long with the curriculum designed to go along with SonForce Kids: *Agents in Action*, a 13-lesson adventure for children ages 3-12. The thrill of accomplishing daily missions for God as His special agents will challenge children to live courageously as His disciples. Distribute information about the course to each student during VBS. *Agents in Action* is available from Gospel Light.

>> In the fall, when it is time to register children for the coming year's Sunday School classes, send an invitation to parents and children. Be sure to include service times, directions to the Sunday School classrooms and information about other classes for children and adults. Include the name and phone number of someone to be contacted for more information.

Follow Up on Administrative Issues

>> Pray for the follow-up efforts and thank God for His work in your VBS program.

>> Express appreciation to all workers. See suggestions for showing appreciation to your staff in "Follow Up with Your Staff" on page 37.

>> Have staff perform an evaluation of your VBS program. See suggestion under "Follow Up with Your Staff" on page 37.

>> See that supplies are packed, labeled and stored for future use.

>> Compile and file all records, receipts and publications.

>> Create a "debriefing file" complete with your checklists, communication records, personnel lists, etc.

>> While the events of VBS are still fresh in your mind, fill out the Questionnaire on pages 103 and 104 of this book. Also create a personal record of how problems were solved and how to avoid similar ones in the future. Include notes of necessary adjustments in schedules, additional supplies needed, etc. Write down good ideas for next year's program. Make a copy for your church files and keep the original for yourself.

>> File names and addresses of workers to be contacted next year.

Follow Up in Your Church

Don't let the efforts of your VBS vanish as soon as the program ends. There will be many people in your church who are interested in knowing the status of your VBS program. People who have been supporting the program through prayers and contributions deserve to know the results.

>> Show a video or slideshow of VBS activities before, during or after worship services. Play music from *SonForce Kids CD* or have students and team members sing VBS songs to accompany the video or slideshow.

>> Publish an encouraging announcement in your church bulletin. Report on the average attendance, the number of unchurched children who attended, the number of volunteers, important decisions that were made, the status of your missions project and any other exciting information about your VBS program. You may also want to include a word of thanks to all who were involved and list their names.

>> Ask older students to fill out a VBS evaluation, asking what they liked best, what they liked least and what they would do differently. In the bulletin, print up some of the positive comments.

>> Make a video, interviewing a variety of kids about their VBS experience. Show video before, during or after a worship service.

>> Ask permission to have a few volunteers or students share their VBS experiences with the congregation during upcoming church services.

>> Arrange to have a group of students sing one or two VBS songs at your worship services following VBS.

>> Leave decorations and samples of your crafts in the rooms for church members to see. Visitors who attended VBS or the Closing Program will feel more at ease returning to familiar surroundings.

>> Design a bulletin board showing photographs and samples of lessons that were taught at VBS.

>> Publish a more in-depth report for your next church newsletter. Include a thank-you to all volunteers and list their names.

Follow Up with Your Staff

One way to keep volunteers excited and geared up for the future is to take the time to recognize them for their efforts. Volunteers often feel unnoticed

STEP-BY-STEP PLANNING GUIDE

and quickly grow tired of giving their time and energy to the church. Let your volunteers know you appreciate them.

>> Mail thank-you notes to every VBS volunteer.

>> Honor volunteers at the Closing Program with a small gift and/or a certificate of appreciation. Full-color certificates are available from Gospel Light. Reproducible certificates are in *Reproducible Resources*.

>> Invite volunteers to a breakfast, brunch or lunch the day after the Closing Program.

>> Ask your volunteers for their evaluation of your VBS. You may want to give them an addressed and stamped envelope to mail responses to you.

>> Encourage volunteers to participate in next year's VBS and discuss with them ways to improve your VBS efforts.

>> Include a general note of thanks and a list of VBS volunteers in the church newsletter or bulletin.

>> Make a memory book with photos, anecdotes and other quotes from VBS. Include an address section with names, e-mail and street addresses of team members. Include an area for team members to add student information in order to keep in touch throughout the year.

Follow Up with Prayer

When you think you've done all the follow-up you can possibly do, there is one final step—prayer. Prayer is the most important element in your follow-up efforts. Share the ideas below with your Prayer Leader (see p. 28) and encourage your VBS prayer team and volunteers to continue praying throughout the year.

>> Praise God for giving you the strength and the opportunity to serve Him through VBS.

>> Praise God for your faithful volunteers.

>> Praise God for, and continue to pray for, the children who came to your VBS and those who made decisions for Christ during VBS.

>> Pray for continued spiritual growth in the lives of your VBS students.

>> Pray for the follow-up efforts of your VBS leaders and helpers.

>> Pray that your church will continue to grow through your VBS outreach.

>> Pray that with God's guidance, volunteers will find a meaningful place of ministry.

>> Pray that God would give you rest and the guidance needed to pursue future areas of ministry.

>> Pray for next year's VBS.

And Don't Forget Yourself!

Doctors, time-management experts and experienced ministry leaders agree—the best thing you can do after a period of stress or extreme busyness is to take time off to recuperate. Even the best VBS preparation and training in the world cannot prevent a director from feeling a little "fried" at times. Taking time off is good for your physical and mental well-being and can do much to strengthen your spiritual walk.

In Mark 1:35-39 Jesus Himself withdrew to a solitary place after a busy time of ministry. Retreating and allowing yourself to spend extra time with the Lord can restore your soul. Plan to simply recuperate in a solitary place, alone or with your family. You deserve it! And when you return to ministry, you will have the strength and insight to face your next challenge.

SAFETY FIRST!

PART OF PREPARING FOR VBS INCLUDES DEALING WITH POTENTIAL SAFETY CONCERNS.

39

SAFETY FIRST!

Part of preparing for VBS includes dealing with potential safety concerns. Be sure to consult your church's current safety policies for children's ministry programs as you develop your VBS safety plan.

Opening and Closing Assemblies

Opening and closing assembly times are great fun and certainly generate excitement and enthusiasm. (See the *Assemblies and Skits Production Guide* for help in planning assemblies.) These assemblies also provide the framework for parents to drop their children off before and pick children up after VBS. Resist the temptation to allow the children to disperse on their own. Check to see if your church has already established procedures for dropping off and picking up children from ministry programs. Here are some suggestions to help you develop your procedures for checking children in and out of SonForce Kids.

Dropping Off

>> Make sure students and parents know the names of their classes and Guides and the location where classes gather before the opening assembly. Set up a greeting table near the main entrance of the church. Decorate it to catch the eye of parents and students as they arrive. Especially on the first day, have at the table several volunteers whose only responsibilities are to greet and direct children as well as answer questions from parents.

>> Have name tags available for all children ahead of time. (Name Tag Holders available from Gospel Light.) As parents drop off their children, put name tags on students. Not only will it be much easier to identify the students, but you can keep track of which students have arrived and which students are still to come.

>> Have visible signs indicating classes for children. At the designated gathering place, Guides stand near the signs to welcome students as they arrive.

>> As groups gather, Guides and helpers greet and talk with students, lead them to sing VBS songs, review Bible stories and memory verses, play simple games like I Spy or Simon Says, and generally start the VBS fun! (For more transition tips, see p. 4 of the *Helper Handbook*.)

>> When assembly is ready to begin, each Guide leads group into assembly area. Guides continue to hold signs high so that latecomers will be able to find their groups.

Picking Up

>> Guides lead one group of students at a time to designated pickup location. Guides release children to parents.

>> If parents will pick up children at classrooms or assembly room, station a volunteer at the door. When a parent arrives, the volunteer announces the name of the child to be dismissed. Only that child is allowed to leave the building.

>> In a small church, you may be able to set up a drive-through pickup area. Place one volunteer at the drive-through area and one inside the assembly area, each with walkie-talkies. When a parent arrives, the outside volunteer calls inside to the volunteer who makes an announcement, dismissing the student to his or her parent. A volunteer at the door ensures only children whose names have been called are dismissed.

>> If children are kept inside the assembly area while waiting for parents to arrive, be sure to have fun activities for children. These activities may be led by the age-level Guides and helpers or the assembly leader. Consider watching the skit DVD again, playing Bible-story review or memory verse games, having volunteers read theme-related books, singing VBS songs or playing simple group games. Keep the fun going until the last student leaves!

Child and Parent Identification

Many churches have developed a system for child identification that ensures children's safety and that they are only released to approved adults. Teachers are then protected from parent complaints and from legal action in instances of custody disputes.

Consider these ideas for a child identification system, choosing one that best fits your church. You can make your own tags or coupons or purchase commercially made child/parent identification systems. Contact your local Christian bookstore for possible sources.

>> **Coupon with Date and Child's Name**—Coupon is given to parent when the child is checked in. Only the person with the coupon is allowed to pick up the child at the end of the session.

>> **Number ID**—Card or paper with date and number assigned to the child. A tag with the corresponding number may also be attached to the child's name tag.

>> **Wallet-Sized, Permanent Identification Cards**—These cards, with parents' and children's names and personal family identification number, can be given to parents. A child is only released to an adult who shows the identification card.

>> **Photo ID**—take photos of each child with his or her parents. Mount photos on a bulletin board near the entrance to each room. Have an instant camera available to photograph visitors.

>> **Parent Designation**—Provide a section on the check-in form in which the parent writes the name of the person who will be picking up the child. Person picking up the child would be requested to show identification if not known to the child's teacher.

Preventing Child Abuse

Preventing child abuse by screening all volunteers is only part of your church's responsibility to protect children. (Consider using Internet resources to check volunteers for criminal histories.) It is also the Director's job to make sure that all volunteers are adequately informed about avoiding inappropriate behaviors. Much of this information is given to protect your volunteers from false allegations. Check to see if your church already has an established policy and read the following tips to help you establish your procedures for VBS.

>> **Establish a Buddy/Witness Policy.** Always have at least two adults (18 years of age or older) present in every activity involving children. This means there will always be a witness built into the situation.

>> **Develop an Appropriate Touching Policy.** Think about, talk about and agree upon what is

"appropriate touching" at your church. Kids need love, but it is wise to guard against false accusations over displays of physical affection.

>> **Write down your policies.** Once you've carefully thought through and have established appropriate guidelines, make them a matter of record. Have your policies available for all parents, caregivers and volunteers to review.

Ensuring Safety on Campus

Making sure your facilities are safe inside and out is part of being well prepared. Check every area that will be in use. Things to look for:

>> **Hazards in each classroom and activity area.** Equip with a first-aid kit.

>> **Objects that cause a child to trip.** Make sure all electrical cords are taped down securely. Remove any protruding tree roots or rocks over which someone may trip. Mark with brightly colored flags anything that cannot be removed.

>> **Items that could cause head or eye injuries.** Look for broken items that have sharp edges. Do a walk-through of each area, considering all protruding items that may be directly at children's eye level.

>> **Harmful chemicals or electrical hazards that may be easily accessed.** Inform your church custodian about the areas that will be in use during VBS. Verify that these areas will be safe from such hazards.

>> **Peeling paint, rust or rotted wood that could cause splinters.** Repaint areas where old paint is peeling or rust is forming. Look for areas where children may be exposed to decaying wood and remove it.

>> **Outdoor areas that may be infested by harmful insects.** To protect children from unseen insects, make sure that grass areas will be mowed and trees trimmed prior to your VBS. Encourage students to wear sunscreen and bug spray. Include suggestion to parents in registration materials.

>> **Water, water everywhere.** Throughout your campus, place tables with paper or plastic cups of water for children to drink during activities and transitions. Place trash cans nearby for disposal of cups.

Special Safety Concerns for Early Childhood

Inspect all areas in which early childhood activities will be conducted. In addition to the aforementioned concerns, check the following:

>> Cover all exposed outlets.

>> Remove small items or toys with pieces on which a child could choke. Also verify that snack, craft and game items are safe from choking hazards.

>> Remove plants that are poisonous if ingested. Check on the Internet or with your local garden store if you have any questions.

>> Check the playgrounds for a safe ground cover of sand, mulch, pea gravel or rubber tiles. Sand areas need a minimum depth of 12 inches (30.5 cm) of loose fill. If properly installed, rubber tiles, hardwood fiber/mulch and safety-tested rubber mats are also options for playground surfaces. All ramps, platforms and bridges should have guardrails with slats less than 3½ inches (9 cm) or more than 9 inches (23 cm) apart. Guardrails and protective barriers should be at least 29 inches (73.5 cm) high.

Dealing with Sick or Injured Children

Prepare a first-aid station or at least have a first-aid kit in an accessible location, such as your church office. Children's registration forms need to be located with the first-aid station. Check to see that the station or kit is well stocked with the following items: adhesive bandages in a variety of sizes, antibacterial ointment, sterile gauze pads, first-aid tape, ipecac syrup, thermometer, disposable gloves, tweezers and a first-aid manual. Post the phone numbers for the nearest poison-control center, fire station and police station where they can be easily seen. Keep an ice pack in a nearby freezer or purchase ice packs that need no refrigeration. You may also want to provide a comfortable place for a child to lie down if needed.

Have a volunteer who is trained in first-aid be the "on-call nurse" in case he or she is needed. Ask the volunteer to review all of the registration forms and clearly mark the cards of children who have a potential health problem and notify Snack Leader of any food allergies. Make sure there is a working phone near your first-aid station so that the volunteer can call emergency workers and parents or caregivers in case of an emergency.

SPECIAL EVENTS

ADD A DAY, A WEEK OR A SUMMER OF FUN TO YOUR SONFORCE KIDS EXPERIENCE!

43

SPECIAL EVENTS

Imagine the impact on children's lives in your community if you expand SonForce Kids outside your congregation or beyond five days! Extra days can give your children special opportunities to deepen relationships and apply what they are learning about God's love. Add a day, a week or a summer of fun to your SonForce Kids experience! For even more ideas about expanding SonForce Kids, read the missions and service ideas on pages 64-65.

Field Trips

Before taking groups of children away from church property, be sure to have parents complete and sign permission and medical-release forms similar to those on the *Director's Guide CD-ROM* (see p. 88).

>> **Mission: Munch** Plan a picnic at a local park. Some workers stay at the picnic site to prepare food and set up decorations, while other helpers gather with children in another part of the park. Children follow clues that take them to different attractions in the park (zoo, rose garden, playground, etc.) before ending up at the picnic site where everyone enjoys the prepared lunch.

>> **Law and Order** If possible, arrange a visit to a local law-enforcement agency, PAL program, etc. If a member of your congregation is a detective, ask him or her to describe to children some of the investigative techniques they use or gadgets and tools that help with investigations.

>> **It's a Technical World** Arrange a tour of a business that uses technology in its operations (print shop, bottling plant, factory, etc.). Discuss how technology has changed the way things are done in that field. When you return to your church, students use recyclables and other art materials to create a special-agent gadget. Students show and tell about their gadgets.

Events at Church

>> **Movie with a Mission** Just before school is out for the summer, post flyers around your town to advertise the showing of a special-agent movie appropriate for all ages. After the movie, divide into intergenerational groups of five or six people. Groups decide on a favorite scene from the movie and act it out for the other groups. Provide snacks and information about your VBS program.

>> **Twinkle Twinkle** At an all-church gathering, meet in an open outside area (playing field, parking lot, etc.). Everyone brings lawn chairs, camp chairs or blankets to sit on. Make sure there are as few lights on as possible. Ask a local expert to identify different stars and constellations and talk about them. Provide some binoculars and if possible, telescopes, for better viewing. Serve cocoa and consider a campfire to gather around and roast marshmallows.

>> **Serving Together** At an all-church gathering, divide the group into intergenerational teams of six to ten people. Ask each team to come up with a team name and provide team name tags for them to decorate. Serve snacks made from recipes in the *Recreation and Snack Center Guide* or other favorite recipes. Teams brainstorm and plan a project they can do to serve their church family: picking up papers left in sanctuary after church services, helping with landscaping, picking up trash on church campus, sending thank-you notes to pastors and Sunday School teachers, serving as a welcome team to greet visitors, etc. Teams come back together and share their plans.

>> **Special-Agent Service** Dedicate a weekly worship service to promote VBS. Here are some suggestions for the service: Introduce the SonForce Kids theme,

SPECIAL EVENTS

show a video or slideshow of previous VBS programs, show the *Preview DVD*, ask former VBS staff and students to talk about ways their participation in VBS has had an impact in their lives, etc. After the service, volunteers and students can sign up at a table set up in a central location.

>> **Summer Curriculum** Keep the spirit of VBS alive all summer long with the curriculum designed to go along with SonForce Kids: *Agents in Action*, a 13-lesson adventure for children ages 3-12. The thrill of accomplishing daily missions for God as His special agents will challenge children to live courageously as His disciples. Use this course as a second-hour program on Sundays, a midweek evening program or any time you work with kids. You and your students will enjoy the flexible format and the variety of activities offered. *Agents in Action* is available from Gospel Light.

Preview Event

Publicize your upcoming VBS by having a promotional Preview Event. This event is a great opportunity to reach out to children and families in your community and to build enthusiasm for VBS among your church's congregation.

The Preview Event includes games, activities and snacks—all related to SonForce Kids VBS. Admission is free. In this informal atmosphere, unchurched parents will feel comfortable visiting your church with their children and will appreciate the good time you provide at no cost. And most importantly, children won't want to miss out on all the fun they will have at your VBS.

Your primary goal at the Preview Event is to motivate the parents and children to enroll in your upcoming VBS program. Schedule your event two to four weeks before VBS. There are several things you can do to ensure that your promotional day leads to meaningful publicity for your VBS.

Staffing

>> Each activity needs at least one adult or youth helper to be in charge. Encourage helpers to dress in theme-related clothing.

>> Ask individual families or adult Sunday School classes or small groups in your church to organize a booth for the Preview Event.

>> Have several helpers and/or the skit characters greet parents and encourage children to try any activity that is low on participation.

Setup

Transform your church parking lot (and/or lawn) into a special-agent training facility with games, activities and snacks. Designate each activity area with colored chalk; an awning, stakes and rope; or even booths. Tents and awnings can be used for appropriate activities. Add a thematic touch by using metallic paints and fabrics, or paint large special-agent objects (binoculars, magnifying glasses, thumbprints, briefcases, cell phones, cameras and other high-tech objects) on structures.

Registration and Information Booth

Set up a tent or table near the entrance to your Preview Event. At this site, parents may register their children for VBS.

Give each child a Preview Event Pass (on this page) that will allow him or her to participate in all activities

PREVIEW EVENT PASS
- Special-Agent Go-Go Juice
- Spicy Spy Popcorn
- Laser Beam Security
- Disguise Shop
- Training Course
- Robot Relays
- Glow Jewelry
- Robo-Photo Stop

This sample is available as a full-size, color electronic file on the *Director's Guide CD-ROM*.

SPECIAL EVENTS

and refreshments, and a small gift such as a button to wear. When children participate in an activity, they get their passes punched or receive a sticker on the space marked for that activity.

Note: This pass can also be given out in advance at Sunday School, a park, a shopping center or door-to-door, etc., to promote SonForce Kids VBS.

Special-Agent Snacks

Set up a refreshment center and serve any or all of the following snacks and drinks:

Pizza in Disguise Children place a small tortilla on a sheet of waxed paper, spread with pizza or spaghetti sauce and cover with a half cup of grated mozzarella and cheddar cheeses. Then they lay a slice of turkey or ham and optional toppings such as olives, sliced peppers, tomatoes, mushrooms, etc. on top. Children fold ends and roll up tortillas like burritos. Optional: Place pizzas in microwave oven for 30 seconds to soften and melt cheese.

Watermelon Stars Use a cookie cutter to cut star shapes from 1-inch (2.5-cm) thick slices of seedless watermelon. Insert a craft stick into each star and set the pops on a foil-lined baking sheet. Cover the stars with another sheet of foil and freeze for 1 hour or until firm.

Crunchy Munchy Cut celery into sticks; wash and dry. Spread cream cheese in each and top with granola. Press granola down into cheese. Add raisins, if desired.

Red-Alert Shake In a blender place 2 cups strawberry ice cream, 2 cups milk, 1 cup vanilla yogurt, 2 large bananas, 1½ tsp. vanilla extract, 4 drops red food coloring. Blend until creamy. Makes 6 servings.

Spicy Spy Popcorn Place 10 cups popped popcorn in a large bowl. In a small bowl, mix 1 tablespoon taco seasoning with ¼ cup melted butter. Add ¼ cup grated Cheddar or Colby cheese, and then stir into warm popcorn. Makes 10 cups.

SPECIAL EVENTS

Special-Agent Go-Go Juice Provide several flavors of frozen juice concentrate. Allow concentrate to soften. For each serving, spoon some concentrate into a tall glass. Pour in seltzer and gently stir to mix. Drop in a few ice cubes.

Starry Night Children spread chocolate frosting on graham crackers and top with candy sprinkles.

Asteroids In a medium bowl, combine 1 cup creamy or chunky style peanut butter, 1 cup powdered milk, 1¼ cups sugar and 1 cup honey. Pull off walnut-sized pieces, roll into balls and set on waxed paper. Refrigerate until firm or roll in shredded coconut, chopped peanuts, miniature chocolate chips or other miniature candies before chilling. Makes 24 to 30 asteroid snacks.

Activities

Special-Agent Identification Have someone handy with graphic arts create several large pictures of members of your church staff or celebrities (local, national or international). Include disguises such as fake mustaches, glasses, wigs, etc. that have been added to the picture. Tape a sheet of paper underneath each image. Participants write down their guess as to who is in the picture. First person to guess each image correctly receives a prize.

Satellite Scenes Visit a website such as www.terraserver.microsoft.com or www.maps.google.com to find satellite images of different well-known locations in your town, the country and/or the world. Print the images and enlarge on a photocopier. Post images in a hallway or gathering place. Tape a sheet of paper underneath each image. Participants write down their guess as to the location in the picture. First person to guess each image correctly receives a prize.

SPECIAL EVENTS

Laser-Beam Security In a room or a hallway, tape lengths of yarn from one side to the other, simulating laser beams. Thread a jingle bell onto one end of each yarn length before taping. Put up a large sign saying, "Warning: Security laser beams. Don't touch or alarm will sound." Players carefully navigate their way through the room or hallway, stepping over or ducking under yarn "beams." (Note: Don't try this in a main hallway where large numbers of people must travel *en masse*.)

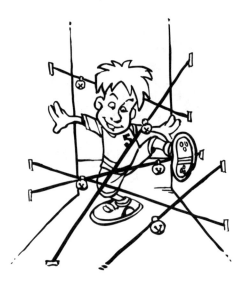

Instant Planetarium Paint the inside of a large cardboard box black. Remove flaps from one end of box, place on floor so that opening is to the side and tape a length of thick black fabric (such as terry cloth or velour) over opening. Using a nail, poke holes through all sides of box and length of fabric. Children sit in box and drop fabric over opening to see "stars" all around. Or do this activity in a dark room, using an electronic home planetarium.

Glow Jewelry Provide glow bracelets, necklaces and key chains along with a variety of beads for kids to make their own jewelry. Purchase glow-in-the-dark beads in a craft store or fishing supply store or make your own by painting wooden beads with glow-in-the-dark paint.

Lemon-Juice Rocket Do this activity outside. Either follow the directions to do a demonstration or guide children to make their own rockets. First, tear a paper towel into strips and attach strips to the top of a cork with tape. (Note: Make sure cork fits snugly into the opening of a 1-liter bottle.) The paper strips make the cork look more like a rocket when it blasts off. Then, put a teaspoon of baking soda in the middle of a square of toilet paper and fold to make a small packet. Put a funnel into the opening of a 1-liter bottle. Pour a half inch of lemon juice into the bottle, and then add water until bottle is a bit less than halfway full. Put on safety glasses. Drop baking soda packet into bottle, quickly close bottle with the cork, shake bottle and stand back for liftoff. (White vinegar may be used instead of lemon juice.)

SPECIAL EVENTS

Get a Clue! Set up a series of clues to locations all over your church campus. Use codes, riddles or extreme close-up photos—or some of each—to create your clues. At the final destination, have a helper hand out prizes.

Blind Boxes Remove the flaps from a medium cardboard box. Turn the box on its side and cut holes in either side. Make sure holes are big enough for participants to put their hands through and move freely. Place a variety of objects on a table next to box. Participants take their place behind the box, where they can no longer see the objects on the table, and place hands in either hole. Hand an object to the participant. If participant is able to identify the object in less than a minute, he or she wins a prize. (Adjust time according to the age and ability of the participant.) If object is not identified, hand child another object until he or she receives a prize.

Robo-Photo Stop On a large piece of cardboard, paint a robot or two. Where the robot face(s) would be, cut a hole(s). Photograph children placing their faces through hole(s). After photos develop or are printed, place in a fun frame (theme-related Photo Frame available from Gospel Light.).

Training Course Set up an obstacle course. Use playground equipment such as swings, slides and balance beams, or create your own obstacles. Some suggestions would be to include a "moon walk" where students walk across an inflated air mattress; throw a ball through a hula hoop suspended from a tree; and a refrigerator box turned on its side that children must crawl through.

SPECIAL EVENTS

Robot Relays Tape large rubber gloves to the ends of two 12-inch (30.5-cm) lengths of dryer hose, one glove per hose. Tape other ends of hose over sleeves of an adult-sized shirt to make a robot shirt. Make two. Place each shirt, a pair of adult-sized rubber boots and a pair of tongs in a pile. Make two such piles next to a starting line. Place a similar number of small objects (toy cars, people or animals; bits of hardware such as large bolts, hinges and sockets; balls; beanbags; etc.) in two large bowls or other containers next to clothing piles. Place two more bowls or containers approximately 20 feet (6 m) away. Form two teams. Teams remove their shoes and line up behind clothing piles. At your signal, the first child in each line puts on robot shirt and boots, and uses tongs to pick up an object from the bowl. Children then make their way to other bowl, deposit object and return to team. When child reaches the team, he or she removes robot shirt and boots and hands them along with tongs to the next child who then takes a turn. First team to move all the objects wins prizes.

>> Use some of the activity ideas from the "Preview Event" article beginning on page 45 to create an unforgettable event for your church and community.

>> Show a "SonForce Kids Highlights" video or slideshow of everyone participating in various VBS activities.

>> Interview several students about their VBS experiences.

>> Have students recite Joshua 1:9.

>> Record a Bible story and pantomime the parts of the story.

>> Present the Closing Program Skit (see script in *Assemblies and Skits Production Guide*, pp. 40-42).

>> Provide snacks from the *Recreation and Snack Center Guide* or other refreshments.

>> Guide families on tours of the classrooms. The team members in their rooms can explain the activities in which students participated during the week. Display some of the objects students made or worked with during VBS.

>> Ask your senior pastor or other member of the pastoral staff to give a brief welcome and an invitation to attend your church's worship services and Sunday School.

>> Set aside a place for kids to get autographs from each other, team members and/or skit characters.

>> In a discreet place, set up an area where people can stop by and place prayer requests and/or pray with a volunteer.

Closing Program

The Closing Program is the culmination of your entire VBS program. It may also be your best opportunity for forming relationships with parents of unchurched children. The program is designed to recap the fun events of the week as well as the plan of salvation, giving children and their families the opportunity to hear and respond to the good news of Jesus Christ. This event is one your children, their parents and your team members will long remember!

Your Closing Program may include any of the following ideas:

PUBLICITY GUIDE

GET THE NEWS OUT FAR AND WIDE—LET EVERYONE KNOW ABOUT SONFORCE KIDS VBS AT YOUR CHURCH!

PUBLICITY GUIDE

Build VBS Interest Within the Church

>> **Bulletin Insert** Announce your VBS dates, provide information about registration, recruit staff and promote your VBS by using bulletin inserts.

>> **Preview DVD** Show the "SonForce Kids Preview" from the *Preview DVD* at children's church or other ministry programs; during a worship service; at Bible studies or prayer meetings; in church lobby, patio or other public area before and/or after church; etc.

>> **VBS Video/Slideshow** Show video footage or slideshows from your church's last VBS program.

>> **Posters** Display posters in a variety of locations around your church.

>> **Sunday School Visits** Give VBS Coloring Posters to children to color and display completed posters in church foyer or other high-traffic area. Visit classes to distribute SonForce Kids T-Shirts, Plastic Tote Bags or Theme Buttons.

>> **Church Website** Add information on SonForce Kids to your church website. Or sign up for an inexpensive, easy-to-use SonForce Kids website from www.myvbs.com (free with purchase of the Super Starter Pack).

>> **Information Booth** Decorate a booth in the church lobby to recruit team members and to preregister children. Display SonForce Kids T-Shirts, Plastic Tote Bags, Theme Buttons, Bookmarks and sample crafts. Make Invitation Postcards and Promotional Flyers available for families to give to prospective students and their families. (See the reproducible sample registration card on p. 34.)

>> **Theme Buttons and SonForce Kids T-Shirts** Have Sunday School teachers, church staff, VBS team members and preregistered students wear VBS items in the weeks leading up to VBS.

>> **SonForce Kids Skits** Present one or more of the SonForce Kids skits (see *Assemblies and Skits Production Guide* and *The Asteroid Incident Skit DVD*) during worship services or other congregational events.

>> **Music** Play songs from *SonForce Kids CD* in Sunday School and use as special music in worship services for several weeks before VBS, or have team members sing a SonForce Kids song.

Reach Out to Children from the Community

>> **Outdoor Banner or Sign** Hang the SonForce Kids Outdoor Banner in a visible place outside your church or paint a large sign.

>> **Posters** Mount posters (Theme Posters and/or completed Coloring Posters) in businesses frequented by children and their families (grocery stores, laundromats, malls, etc.) and on community bulletin boards.

>> **Invitation Postcards** Mail personal Invitation Postcards to last year's VBS students who do not attend your church. Enclose an audiocassette or CD of this year's songs. (CDs are available in a pack of 10 as *Student Music Packs,* an inexpensive alternative to making copies on your own.)

>> **Promotional Flyers and/or Doorknob Hangers** Distribute your personalized invitations throughout the neighborhood.

>> **SonForce Kids Skits** Present a brief skit and announcement in parks and neighborhoods (see *Assemblies and Skits Production Guide*). A CD player can be used to play songs from *SonForce Kids CD* to help attract a crowd.

>> **Radio** Use one or both promotional radio spots on the *SonForce Kids CD* to publicize your VBS over local radio stations. After a SonForce Kids introduction, there is background music over which you can announce details about your church's VBS.

>> **Newspaper, Television and Other Media** Purchase ad space or use community news space. Use the sample News Release (see p. 53) as the basis for a newspaper article about your VBS. Include names of leaders and a photo of some of your staff or the skit characters (Miss Newton, Inez Halley, Jack Oort, Edward Clark Felton and Robot) for an interesting photo!

Publicity Pieces

>> Bulletin Cover/Insert or Promotional Flyer*
>> Clip Art Sheet*
>> Coloring Poster*
>> Doorknob Hanger*
>> Invitation Postcard*
>> Iron-On T-Shirt Transfer*
>> Large Theme Poster*
>> Outdoor Banner
>> Plastic Tote Bags*
>> *Preview DVD*
>> Small Theme Poster*
>> SonForce Kids T-Shirts
>> *Student Music Packs*
>> Theme Bookmark*
>> Theme Button
>> *SonForce Kids Reproducible CD*

*Free in Director's Sample Pack

PUBLICITY GUIDE

>> **Preview Event** Stimulate VBS interest by holding a Preview Event a week or two before VBS begins. Invite 4- through 12-year-olds and their parents for an afternoon of games, refreshments, crafts, skits and other fun activities (see "Preview Event" on pp. 45-50).

>> **Preregistration Bonuses** Give a VBS Theme Button, Bookmark or Skin Decal to each student who pre-registers. Give other VBS goodies to the first 10 (or 20, or . . .) students who preregister. (Theme Buttons, Bookmarks, Skin Decals and other prizes are available from Gospel Light.)

>> **Direct Mail** Customize the flyer on the *Director's Guide CD-ROM*. Send it to every family in your community. Have prizes available for children who return flyer to Registration Booth.

>> **Prizes** During VBS, give T-shirts or other prizes to students who bring three or more friends.

>> **Parents' Class** Invite parents of VBS students to one or more adult classes held during VBS. Include a get-acquainted coffee time with a variety of special-interest presentations (child development, managing stress, discipline, etc.). Or offer an informal Bible study time. Our recommended adult Bible study for this adult class is *Wired That Way* (see VBS order blank).

Publicity Materials

Customize these publicity materials to promote your VBS program.

News Release

Send the News Release to the city desk of local newspapers, or use it as a script for radio or television interviews. Adapt the information to fit your church's situation. Send an abbreviated version to your local television station, weekly shopper and appropriate radio stations.

Direct Mail Flyer

Use the Direct Mail Flyer to inform families in your church about VBS as well as for outreach to families in the community. As needed, use the electronic file available on the *Director's Guide CD-ROM* to adapt it to your church's VBS format (Intergenerational VBS, day camp, Backyard Bible School, etc.) and anything else you wish to customize. You may wish to add fun SonForce Kids art (clip art available in Director's Sample Pack, *Reproducible Resources* or on *Clip Art & Publicity CD-ROM*, www.myvbs.com and www.gospellight.com) to further customize your flyer.

Invitations

Use these fun and attractive postcards to promote different aspects of your VBS program. In addition, e-postcards are available at www.myvbs.com.

Tip: When you send the Follow-Up Postcard, consider enclosing a brochure describing church programs for all ages.

These samples are available as full-size, color electronic files on the *Director's Guide CD-ROM*.

© 2007 GOSPEL LIGHT. PERMISSION TO PHOTOCOPY GRANTED. SONFORCE KIDS *DIRECTOR'S GUIDE*

PUBLICITY GUIDE

PUBLICITY CALENDAR

16 Weeks Before:
>> Plan publicity with Director and order publicity materials.

>> Put VBS date announcements in your church bulletin. Use a **Bulletin Insert** or text such as "SonForce Kids Vacation Bible School will be held June 19-23. Mark your calendars now!"

12 Weeks Before:
>> Show a "Recruiting Commercial" from the *Preview DVD* in church services and adult Sunday School classes to develop enthusiasm and to recruit leaders. Show "SonForce Kids Preview" from the DVD in children's Sunday School classes.

>> Put another VBS announcement in your church bulletin. Use a **Bulletin Insert** or text such as "This year's Vacation Bible School, SonForce Kids, will set kids on an out-of-this-world adventure to discover how to have courage as God's special agents! Songs, skits, crafts, games, Bible studies and snacks—all make VBS a can't-miss experience. Dates: (insert dates). Cost: $ (insert cost). Sign-ups begin (insert date)."

8 Weeks Before:
>> Hang **Outdoor Banner**.

>> Begin placing **Posters** in church building and community.

>> Photocopy and distribute **Coloring Posters**.

>> Put another VBS announcement in your church bulletin. Use a **Bulletin Insert** or text such as "Plan now to get your summer off to a great start! This year's exciting VBS program is (insert dates). Children will love being God's special agents at SonForce Kids as they learn how to have courage and serve God. Sign-ups begin (insert date)."

4 Weeks Before:
>> Distribute **Theme Buttons and/or SonForce Kids T-Shirts** to all Sunday School teachers and VBS team members to wear to church from now through the end of VBS.

>> Mail **Invitation Postcards** to prospective students and last year's attendees from outside your church.

>> Deliver **Promotional Flyers and/or Doorknob Hangers** throughout neighborhood. Instant e-postcards are available through www.myvbs.com.

>> Provide final details regarding preregistration in your church bulletin using a **Bulletin Insert** or text such as "Don't let this summer's biggest adventure pass you by. Sign up TODAY for SonForce Kids, On a Mission for God, this year's exciting Vacation Bible School program. Dates: (insert dates). Cost: $(insert cost). Invite a friend!" Place similar announcements each week prior to your VBS.

>> Display completed **Coloring Posters**.

>> Arrange to air VBS Promotional Spot on local **Radio** station.

>> Use the News Release (see page 53) and the sample ad on Clip Art Sheet to make contact with local **Newspaper, Television and Other Media**.

>> Contact each family in the community using **Direct Mail**.

This calendar is available as a full-size, color electronic file on the *Director's Guide CD-ROM*.

NEWSLETTERS

KEEP YOUR STAFF AND THE PARENTS OF YOUR VBS STUDENTS UP-TO-DATE WITH THESE CUSTOMIZABLE DAILY NEWSLETTERS.

NEWSLETTERS

Keep your staff and the parents of your VBS students up-to-date with these daily newsletters. Each one is available in customizable form on the *Director's Guide CD-ROM*. Read the existing newsletters and then insert information and photos specific for your VBS or add clip art. (Clip art is also available on our websites, www.gospellight.com and www.myvbs.com, and the *Clip Art & Publicity CD-ROM*.) Replace or revise the suggested announcements. Fill in the names of the crafts kids did at your VBS. It's your newsletter—make it personal!

Both the Staff and Parent Newsletters have important information for each VBS session: Daily Mission, Focus, Memory Verse, Bible Story reference. They also include reminders, announcements and previews of things to come. The Staff Newsletter also includes prayer requests and praises. The Parent Newsletter includes a recap of the day's activities and conversation starters to get kids talking about what they did—a great way to reinforce their learning as well as developing the parent-child relationship.

Use one or both types of newsletters to keep the people so important to the success of your VBS informed of what's going on.

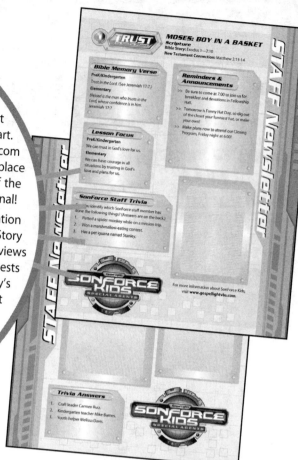
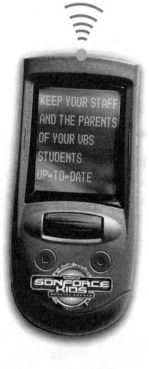

ACTIVITY CENTER GUIDE

THE ACTIVITY CENTER PLAN IS A POPULAR LEARNING FORMAT FOR VBS PROGRAMS.

ACTIVITY CENTER GUIDE

The Activity Center Plan is a popular learning format for VBS programs. Each leader and his or her team specialize in only one part of the lesson. Small groups of students led by Guides rotate among the various activity centers. One room or outside area is designated for each of the activities your program provides.

The Bible Story Center is the core of VBS. Choose from these other centers based on your staff, your facility and the total time available: Opening and Closing Assembly, Crafts, Snacks, Music and Recreation Games, for example. Other centers may include Theme Center, Bible Games or Missions and Service.

Note

Activities are designed to operate best with groups of up to 16 students. Up to 24 students in each center may be accommodated if there are additional teachers and sufficient space.

Small Groups and Guides

Students are assigned to small, permanent groups (six to eight students per Guide or helper and no more than 12 to 16 total students in a group). Each group of students visits each center during each session of the program. Many churches use at least one Guide and one helper to lead each group and travel with the group to each center. (Note: Some churches combine the positions of Guide and Bible Story Leader.)

Leaders

Each leader takes responsibility for one center. The leader remains at the center and instructs each small group as it visits the center. Leaders make adjustments in method and content according to the age level of the students visiting the center (age-level adaptations are included in all *Center Guides*).

Note

The Activity Center Plan is recommended for students in grades 1-6. Preschool and kindergarten children remain in a separate area and do not rotate through activity centers. Preschoolers learn best in the security of a familiar classroom (see "Planning Your Early Childhood VBS" beginning on p. 20).

ACTIVITY CENTER GUIDE

The Activity Center Plan—How It Works

The diagram and sample schedules found on the following pages show how the Activity Center Plan can work in your church. Adjust the schedule according to the number of staff and students in your program.

Opening Assembly

The session begins as all students, leaders and helpers meet together for the opening assembly. This assembly includes a welcome, songs and a skit. Encourage leaders, helpers and other VBS staff to sit with students and participate in the assembly activities.

After the Opening Assembly

Guides and helpers escort their small groups from center to center.

Bible Story Center

The leader tells the Bible story and leads students in a life-application discussion using the *SFA Manuals*.

Theme Center

The leader prepares and leads a theme-related activity that reviews the life application of each day's lesson.

Bible Games Center

The leader prepares and leads a game that reviews the Bible story and/or the Bible memory verse and connects it to students' everyday lives.

Missions and Service Center

The leader plans and supervises the teaching about missions and the missions project or other service projects. (Note: Instead of having a separate center, missions could be a part of your opening assembly time. See "Missions and Service Center" on pp. 63-72.)

Recreation and Snack Center

The Recreation Game Leader prepares and leads the group in high-energy theme-related games. The Snack Leader helps the group in preparing fun theme-related snacks to eat and enjoy.

Music Center

In a large room or outdoor area, the leader instructs each group in a variety of music activities and teaches the SonForce Kids songs. Information for the Music Center Leader is found in the *SonForce Kids Songbook*.

Craft Center

The leader prepares and guides the students in making a craft project. Information for the Craft Center Leader is found in *Special Agent Crafts for Kids*.

Closing Assembly

All groups meet together for a closing assembly which includes announcements, songs and Bible verse review. Guides collect name tags from students. As students leave, have them collect take-home materials from designated areas.

Helpful Hints!

- » Predetermine the route each group will travel, including entrances and exits. Have Guides walk their routes in advance to become familiar with all locations.
- » Establish a signal for letting groups know when it's time to move to the next center. (See "Transitions" under "Bonus Theme Ideas" on p. 10.)
- » Provide labeled tables or other areas where students may leave their belongings throughout the day and pick them up before going home.
- » Set up your centers in classrooms or under tents, awnings or shade trees. Students sit on towels, tarps, mats, blankets or picnic benches.
- » Provide color-coded name tags, bandanas or wristbands to identify groups.
- » Post a large sign to identify each center.
- » Give your centers names appropriate for SonForce Kids: Mission Command (Assembly Room) for Opening and Closing Assemblies and Skits, The Pizza Pod for snacks, Tech Lab for crafts, Trans Port for Bible Story Center. Other centers could be called Communications Bay, SAT-5, etc.

ACTIVITY CENTER GUIDE

Diagram for Sample Activity Center Schedule

ACTIVITY CENTER GUIDE

Activity Center Plan for 36-48 First through Sixth Graders

Sample Three-Hour Schedule

Time	Primary	Middler	Preteen
9:00-9:15	Opening Assembly	Opening Assembly	Opening Assembly
9:20-9:45	Bible Story Center	Craft Center	Music Center
9:50-10:15	Activity Center	Bible Story Center	Craft Center
10:20-10:45	Recreation and Snack Center	Activity Center	Bible Story Center
10:50-11:15	Music Center	Recreation and Snack Center	Activity Center
11:20-11:45	Craft Center	Music Center	Recreation and Snack Center
11:50-12:00	Closing Assembly	Closing Assembly	Closing Assembly

This schedule is available as a full-size, color electronic file on the *Director's Guide CD-ROM*.

ACTIVITY CENTER GUIDE

Activity Center Plan for 72-96 First through Sixth Graders

12-16 children per group (Allow five minutes transition time between centers.)

Centers to set up:
>> Two Bible Story Centers (A and B; one for first-second graders, one for third-sixth graders)
>> Two Craft Centers (A and B; one for first-second graders, one for third-sixth graders)
>> Two Activity Centers (A and B; one for first-second graders, one for third-sixth graders)*
>> One Recreation/Snack Center (third-fourth graders will be in this center at the same time)
>> One Music Center (both groups of first graders and second-third graders will be in this center at the same time)

* Activity Center may include one or more of the following: Theme Center, Bible Games Center or Missions and Service Center.

Sample Three-Hour Schedule

Time	1st Grade (group a)	1st Grade (group b)	2nd Grade	3rd Grade	4th Grade	5th/6th Grade
9:00-9:15	Opening Assembly	Opening Assembly	Opening Assembly	Opening Assembly	Opening Assembly	Opening Assembly
9:20-9:45	Bible Story Center A	Craft Center A	Recreation and Snack Center	Bible Story Center B	Music Center	Craft Center B
9:50-10:15	Activity Center A	Bible Story Center A	Craft Center A	Activity Center B	Bible Story Center B	Recreation and Snack Center
10:20-10:45	Recreation and Snack Center	Activity Center A	Bible Story Center A	Craft Center B	Activity Center B	Music Center
10:50-11:15	Music Center	Music Center	Activity Center A	Recreation and Snack Center	Recreation and Snack Center	Bible Story Center B
11:20-11:45	Craft Center A	Recreation and Snack Center	Music Center	Music Center	Craft Center B	Activity Center B
11:50-12:00	Closing Assembly	Closing Assembly	Closing Assembly	Closing Assembly	Closing Assembly	Closing Assembly

For More than 96 Students: Offer more of each type of center. Centers have the same activities but in different locations. Offer as many as needed so that groups visiting the center have no more than 16 students.

This schedule is available as a full-size, color electronic file on the *Director's Guide CD-ROM*.

MISSIONS AND SERVICE CENTER GUIDE

DOING A MISSIONS PROJECT DURING VBS IS AN EXCELLENT WAY TO COMMUNICATE WHAT IT MEANS TO LIVE FOR CHRIST.

MISSIONS AND SERVICE CENTER

Doing a missions project during VBS is an excellent way to communicate what it means to live for Christ. Students learn how to be special agents for God at VBS. By helping others in the world around them, students have an opportunity to share God's love and put into direct practice what they've learned about serving God.

Your VBS Missions Project

Your missions project can fit into your VBS program in any one of several ways:

>> have a five-minute "Moment for Missions" during your Opening Assembly;

>> teach a longer session in individual classrooms; or

>> set up a Missions Activity Center, visited by individual classes each day.

Choosing a Missions Project

Consider these factors:

>> Visual information about the missionary or special project (such as photos, posters, artifacts, maps, etc.) is important for increasing students' understanding and maintaining their interest.

>> Students respond better to meeting a specific need and tangible goal than to giving to a general fund.

>> Families who do not regularly attend your church will often be most responsive to a project that assists people with physical needs such as food, clothing or medical aid.

>> Your church or denomination may have a designated missionary or a missions project. Ask the pastor of your church for more information.

Missions and Service Ideas

>> **Blast-Off Project** As partners in ministry with Gospel Light Worldwide* (a not-for-profit 501(c)3 ministry), the children in your VBS will help reach children in Egypt with God's amazing love (see pp. 65-66 for project details).

>> **Help-Bot** In your missions center or assembly room, set up a large cardboard box decorated to look like a robot. Use a discarded dryer or large appliance box with a hole cut in the side. Place a medium-sized box on top, paint and print "Help-Bot" on the box. Attach gardening gloves to two lengths of dryer hose and then attach dryer hose to medium box to form robot arms. Wrap construction paper around a coffee can (or other large can) and decorate to look like a face. Twist wire and attach to can lid (see sketch).

Explain to students that one way we can serve God is by showing kindness and com-

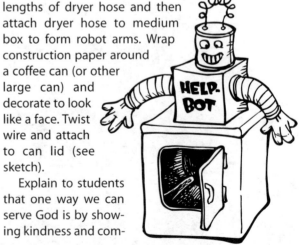

* Gospel Light Worldwide is a not-for-profit 501(c)3 global literature ministry. Gospel Light Worldwide reserves the right to direct funds to other Bible curriculum projects in the most needy parts of the world.

MISSIONS AND SERVICE CENTER

passion to our less-fortunate neighbors. Have students bring in nonperishable food, clothing or other items for a local shelter or food bank your church supports. Each day kids drop items into the Help-Bot. Students can also help sort the donations into boxes or bags and go with you to deliver them when appropriate.

>> **Crafty Gift** Students prepare materials for crafts to be made by children in a homeless shelter. Include a copy of *Special Agent Crafts for Kids* along with general craft supplies as well as specific supplies for some of the crafts in the book.

>> **Take the Show on the Road** Arrange to perform the Closing Program skit (pp. 40-42 in *Assemblies and Skits Production Guide*) at a local hospital, retirement home or homeless shelter.

>> **Collectable Cans** Students collect aluminum cans or other recyclable materials to raise money for Gospel Light Worldwide, missionaries or another charitable ministry supported by your church.

>> **Fund-Raising Fun** Students work together to plan a car wash or bake sale. Students make flyers and distribute them several days before the event. Students invite parents and other family members to join them in washing cars or making and selling baked goods.

Blast-Off Project: Team Up to Help Egypt's Children

Give your students the opportunity to help children thousands of miles away. As Gospel Light Worldwide's ministry partner, you will help reach thousands of children in Egypt—many for the very first time—with God's love.

Gospel Light Worldwide responds to the needs of the world's children in two ways:

1. It addresses the shortage of books by creating children's Bible teaching materials in languages appropriate to individual countries. Based on Gospel Light's curricula, these age-appropriate materials will be carefully adapted to fit the cultures in which they will be used.

2. It provides systematic and comprehensive training for Sunday School teachers in the effective use of these new materials.

The need for these resources is great. In this project, we will focus on the needs of Egypt's children. Though comprising the largest Christian community of the Middle East, Egypt's Christians are an endangered minority. In response to continuous persecution, thousands have left the country or converted to Islam to escape persecution. However, recent pressure from the United States' Freedom from Religious Persecution Act has resulted in positive changes, including a government crackdown on Islamist militants. These changes create an opportunity to reach Egypt's children with God's Word.

Worldwide, generations of people have lived and died without ever hearing the good news of Jesus Christ. That can change as we teach children about God's love for them. Together we can give the enduring message of hope to Egypt's children, their families and generations to come!

After SonForce Kids VBS, send the money raised to Gospel Light Worldwide*, P.O. Box 3875, Ventura, CA 93006.

Gospel Light Worldwide will send your church/ VBS a special thank-you to remind the children of the important role they played in world missions.

Contact Gospel Light Worldwide at 1-800-737-6071 or online at www.gospellightworldwide.org for more information.

Blast-Off Visual

Your VBS students will watch excitedly as their rocket moves along a path headed toward Earth, getting closer to landing on their fund-raising goal!

On card stock draw and decorate a picture of the

* Gospel Light Worldwide reserves the right to direct donations to the children's Bible-curriculum projects in the most needy parts of the world.

MISSIONS AND SERVICE CENTER

Earth. Include the word "Egypt" written to the side in large letters and show an arrow pointing to Egypt's approximate location. Cut out. Also on card stock, draw a satellite station with the SonForce Kids logo on it. Draw, decorate and cut out a rocket ship from a piece of card stock. (Patterns available on p. 67.)

On a large black or dark blue sheet of poster board, glue Earth picture to the upper right corner. In the lower left corner, glue satellite station. In between the Earth and the satellite station, make a path with glitter glue, leading from the satellite station to Earth. At evenly spaced distances along the path, glue large star cut-outs with metallic or glow-in-the-dark numerals representing dollar amounts, increasing from zero to the fund-raising goal, with the fund-raising goal right next to the Earth. Stick small metallic or glow-in-the-dark stars over the rest of the poster board.

Attach a loop of tape to the back of the rocket ship. Each day, move the rocket ship along the path, showing the amount of money that has been collected. Encourage your kids to reach the goal or even go beyond!

Optional Ideas

>> Collect the offering in gold-painted rocket (see p. 13).
>> Divide your group into two teams (such as the boys versus the girls) to generate enthusiasm! Assign a goal to each team. The team reaching their goal first wins the competition and members receive a small prize (Bookmarks, Theme Buttons, Peel 'n Press Stickers, Skin Decals, Special Agent ID Tags, Blacklight Pens, Agent Sunglasses, Fold-Up Binoculars and Secret Message Scroll Pens are some of the theme-related prizes available from Gospel Light).

Tips for Leaders

>> Each missions activity has been carefully designed to incorporate the VBS theme into the missions project. Adapt the ideas as needed so that they are appropriate for your class size, student age, schedule and facilities.
>> As you do the activities, share information from the "Conversation" section of each activity.
>> Remind children that their offerings will help children just like themselves learn about Jesus.
>> Pray with your students daily for the needs of Egypt's children. As the children gain knowledge about Egypt through the specially designed activities, the prayer time will become more meaningful to them!

Getting Kids and Parents Involved

>> Display a poster with visual aids of the project. Maps and other interesting visuals for many of the featured countries are available online at www.wordirect.com.
>> On the first day of your VBS, explain how the Blast-Off Visual (see p. 65) will be used to show your progress throughout your VBS. Give an update every session.
>> Explain what the students' donations will accomplish in terms they can understand. ("Some of the money we raise will help make books about Jesus. Teachers can use these books to teach children in Egypt about God's love.")
>> Write a letter to parents about the Blast-Off Project, or use the sample on the *Director's Guide CD-ROM*. Send the letter home with students after the first session of VBS. Students will stay excited when the whole family participates.
>> Suggest that students earn money by doing jobs for their parents. Some suggestions are included in the sample parent letter. Another job students can do that will raise money for missions and help our own environment is to collect aluminum cans or other recyclable materials.

Parent Letter

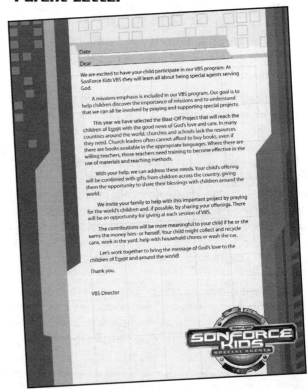

MISSIONS AND SERVICE CENTER

Blast-Off Visual Patterns

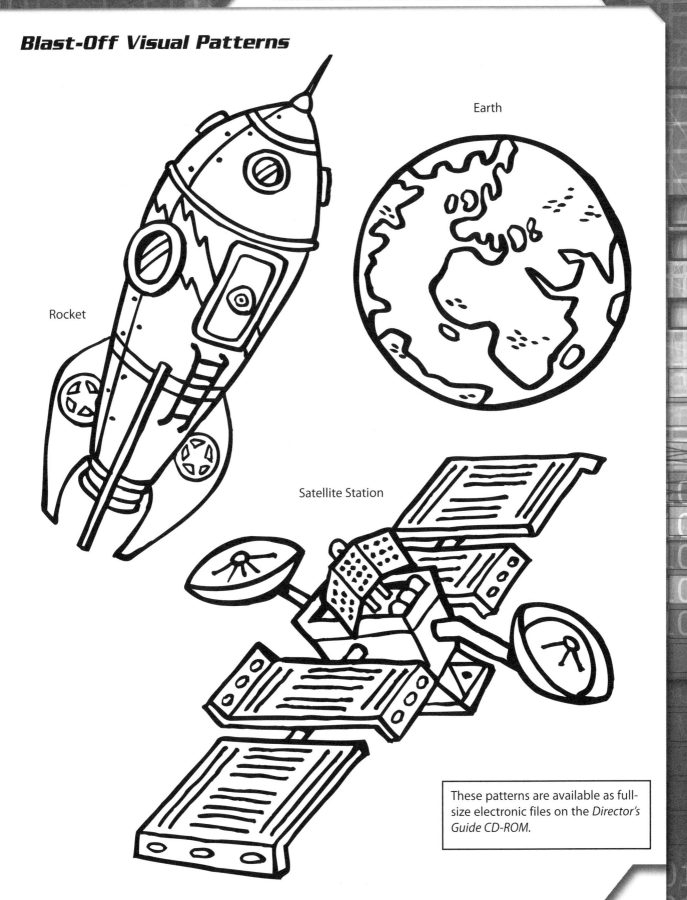

These patterns are available as full-size electronic files on the *Director's Guide CD-ROM*.

MISSIONS AND SERVICE CENTER

Missions Activities

Session 1 >> Paper Papyrus

Materials Checklist
- 9x12-inch (23x30.5-cm) light-colored construction paper
- scissors
- permanent marker
- tub or basin filled with water
- rocks and/or hammers
- clothesline
- clothespins

Preparation: Cut some of the construction paper into ½x9-inch (1.3x23-cm) strips. On another sheet of construction paper, draw vertical lines ½-inch (1.3-cm) apart that begin ½-inch (1.3-cm) from the top and stop ½-inch (1.3-cm) from the bottom (sketch a). Photocopy onto other sheets of construction paper, making one for each student. Attach clothesline in a sunny place, either in- or outdoors.

Procedure: Students cut on lines, leaving ends intact. Then they weave construction-paper strips into the vertical slits they've created. Once woven, students write their names on sheets using permanent marker and then soak sheets in water. Once soaked, each student takes his or her sheet outside and pounds on it with a rock or hammer, pounding both sides (sketch b). Then, students pin sheets to clothesline to dry. (Sheets will be used in Session 2 activity.)

Conversation: **The paper we're making is similar to paper ancient Egyptians made by pounding reeds with rocks. That paper was called papyrus because it was made from plants called papyrus. The tall reeds grow along the Nile River in Egypt. We heard about the Nile River today in our Bible story about Moses. We also heard about how Moses' mother trusted in God's plan for her baby.**

 Today we discovered that we can "TRUST in God's Plans." Because God loves us and has a plan for each of us, we can have courage in all situations. This is good news we can share with the children of Egypt. This year our VBS missions offerings will be used to help children in Egypt learn about God's love and His plans for them. We can help the children of Egypt learn how to become members of God's family!

MISSIONS AND SERVICE CENTER

Session 2 >> Writing in Hieroglyphics

Materials Checklist
>> Paper Papyrus sheets made in Session 1
>> markers

Preparation: Photocopy the Hieroglyph Chart shown on this page, making a copy for each student. (The chart is also available on the *Director's Guide CD-ROM*.)

Procedure: Students use their copy of the Hieroglyph Chart and the Paper Papyrus sheet they made in Session 1 to write their names and any other messages they want.

Conversation: **Ancient Egyptians used a form of writing that uses pictures instead of letters. That form of writing is called "hieroglyphs" and looks like something we might use as a special-agent code!**

Our mission today is to "UNITE with God's People." Uniting together to give offerings to help children in Egypt is one way to complete this mission. We're standing up for the children in Egypt and children all over the world by meeting their need for Sunday School books written in languages they understand. By giving generously, we can all help the children of Egypt learn about God's love and how to they can unite with us by becoming God's people, too!

Hieroglyph Chart

Hieroglyph	Sound	Example	Hieroglyph	Sound	Example	Hieroglyph	Sound	Example
	Short A, Short E, Short O	cat, egg, dog, tall		Soft G, J	judge, jump		OO, Long U	food, rude, cute
	Long A	bake, pail		Hard G	grape		P	pin
	B	bat		H	her		QU	quick
	Soft C, Soft S	mice, sit		Short I, Long I, Hard Y, Y like I	him, hide, yellow, fly		R	run
	Hard C	cat		K	kite		Hard S, Z	days, zebra
	CH	child		L	lake		SH	shark
	D, Soft TH	dog, thumb		M	mother		T, Hard TH	tall, the
	Long E, Y like E	bee, ready		N	Nile		V	vine
	F	fish, phone		Long O, Uh, Short U, W	coat, cook, push, cut, win		X	fox

© 2007 GOSPEL LIGHT. PERMISSION TO PHOTOCOPY GRANTED. SONFORCE KIDS *DIRECTOR'S GUIDE*

MISSIONS AND SERVICE CENTER

Session 3 >> Chapatis and Bean Dip

Materials Checklist

Chapatis
- >> 2 c. whole wheat flour
- >> ½ tsp. salt
- >> 2 tbsp. vegetable oil
- >> ½ c. water
- >> rolling pin
- >> waxed paper
- >> measuring utensils
- >> serving plate
- >> mixing bowl and spoon
- >> pastry brush
- >> electric frying pan
- >> spatula

Optional—
- >> butter, cheese spread, jam or honey

Bean Dip
- >> 1 tomato coarsely chopped
- >> 1 onion coarsely chopped
- >> 2 garlic cloves
- >> 2 tbsp. soy sauce
- >> 4 tbsp. chili powder
- >> 2 tbsp. ground cumin
- >> 2 c. cooked pinto or fava beans
- >> blender
- >> measuring utensils
- >> bowl

Optional—
- >> 1 red hot chili pepper, halved
- >> tortilla chips and/or crackers

Procedure: Gather ingredients for one or both recipes. You may wish to divide class into groups. Make sure the group making chapatis has more members than the group making bean dip.

Chapatis

Students wash hands, then measure flour and salt into a bowl. They measure and add oil, then work it into flour thoroughly with fingers. Children measure and stir in water, then work dough with hands until it holds together. Dough should be kneaded until smooth, about five minutes, in the bowl or on a piece of waxed paper.

Divide dough into 10 to 12 balls. Children roll balls between waxed paper sheets to make thin circles about 7 inches (17.5 cm) in diameter. Students then take dough to an adult helper who brushes oil onto each chapati and places it in electric frying pan set at medium heat. Chapatis cook about one minute on each side. If a chapati puffs, adult helper gently presses down on it with a spatula. Makes 10 to 12 chapatis.

When chapatis cool, students tear off pieces to dip into bean dip. (Optional: Provide butter, cheese spread, jam or honey for students to eat with chapatis.)

Bean Dip

Students wash hands. Under adult supervision, students place tomato, onion, garlic, soy sauce, chili powder and cumin in a blender. (Optional: Older students who might want to try a spicier dip add red hot chili pepper.) Students process mixture on medium speed until smooth, add 1 cup of beans and process until well blended, and then add remaining beans and blend again until smooth. Students place in bowl and serve with chapatis. (Optional: Serve with tortilla chips and/or crackers.) Yields 2 cups.

Conversation: **Chapati** (chuh-PAH-tee) **is eaten in Africa, the Middle East, India and many other places. Egypt is in North Africa. Another popular food in Egypt is bean dip. In our Bible story today, Daniel made the wise choice to only eat foods that would be pleasing to God.**

Today's mission is to "TRAIN for God's Service." We can have courage to make wise choices by training to serve God. One way to serve God is to help other people learn more about Him. By giving money to help the children in Egypt, we're making it possible for them to learn about God and make the wise choice to serve Him!

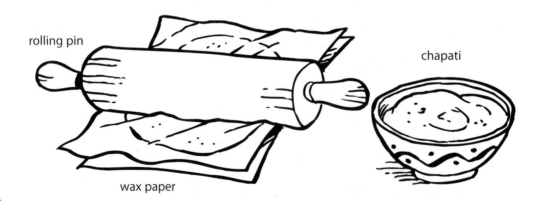

MISSIONS AND SERVICE CENTER

Session 4 >> Stick Race

Materials Checklist

For each student—

>> 4-foot (1.2-m) stick (broom handles, dowels, etc.)

Procedure: Students play a practice round before beginning to eliminate players. Players stand in a large circle, each person about 8 feet (2.4 m) from the next person, facing the middle of the circle. Each player holds a stick upright in the left hand, with one end of the stick on the ground.

At your signal, each player simply opens his or her hand and lets go of his or her own stick, then races to catch the stick of the player to the right before that stick falls and touches the ground. If the stick falls and touches the ground, the player who did not catch it is out, along with the stick. The circle shrinks according to the number of players eliminated in each round. Continue playing until only one player remains. Repeat as time allows.

Conversation: **Just like you, children in Egypt like to play games. Games are only fun if everyone follows the rules. Today our mission is to "FOLLOW in God's Path." That means to obey God's rules. It isn't always easy to obey, but God will give us courage even when it's hard. This week, the money you give will help children in Egypt and all over the world learn about God and His Son, Jesus. When Egypt's children learn that God sent Jesus to die for the wrong things that we do, they can choose to become members of God's family and follow in His path, too.**

Primary Adaptation: Use only one stick. As music plays, hand stick to a student who bangs it on ground twice and then passes it to the next student. Whoever is holding the stick when the music stops is out.

MISSIONS AND SERVICE CENTER

Session 5 >> Paper Pyramid

Materials Checklist
>> card stock
>> sandpaper
>> crayons
>> scissors
>> glue

Optional—
>> samples of Egyptian art

Preparation: Enlarge and photocopy Paper Pyramid Patterns onto card stock and cut out, making one of each pattern for each student. (Patterns are also available on *Director's Guide CD-ROM*.) Enlarge the patterns to make the size pyramid you want. (Optional: Find samples of Egyptian art online or at the library. Place samples in activity area.)

Procedure: On sandpaper, students trace around pyramid side pattern three times, trace around pyramid bottom pattern once and cut out all pieces. Using crayons and pressing hard, students decorate three of their pyramid pieces with drawings of their choosing. (Note: For authentically Egyptian drawings, suggest students draw figures of people so that the bodies are facing forward, but the heads are turned to the side.) (Optional: Students refer to sample of Egyptian art.)

Folding pyramid pieces along the folded lines, students first glue three sides of pyramid together and then glue sides to the bottom.

Conversation: **Egypt is well-known for its magnificent pyramids. People all over the world travel to Egypt to see the pyramids. The pyramid you make today can remind you of our mission to "LEAD Others to God's Promises." Today we've been discussing how we can have courage to lead others to God's promises. The money you've brought for our missions offering will be used to help children in Egypt learn about God's love and promises. We can help the children of Egypt learn the best promise of all—that everyone can become a member of God's family!**

Paper Pyramid Patterns

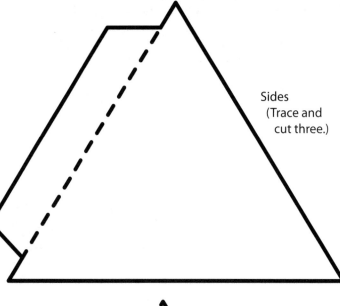

Sides
(Trace and cut three.)

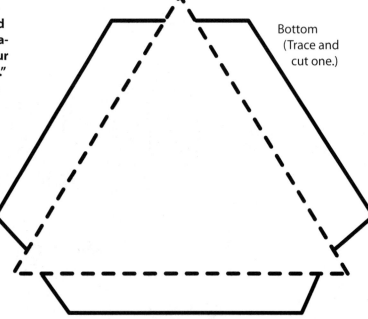

Bottom
(Trace and cut one.)

NURSERY AND TODDLER GUIDE

EVERYTHING YOU NEED TO PROVIDE THE VERY BEST CHILD CARE FOR YOUR VBS WORKERS.

Nursery and Toddler Guide

Providing child care for your volunteers during meetings and at VBS is one of the most over-looked areas in planning a VBS program. However, if you have parents in your church with young children, this is an extremely important issue in recruiting. Parents will want the very best care for their own children while they are volunteering. Therefore, it is a good idea to make your plans for child care while you are still in the recruiting stages. As the Director, you want your VBS team members to be comfortable leaving their little ones in the nursery, knowing they are being well cared for and nurtured. Team members will then freely give their energies to their tasks.

Choosing Caregivers

Depending on the ages your VBS program includes, you may need to provide child care for children anywhere from newborn to five years old. If you expect to have quite a few children in this range, consider asking your Nursery/Toddler Director or a similarly experienced volunteer to help coordinate this area. This person will be responsible for creating a safe and interesting environment with age-appropriate activities and should assist in recruiting other caregivers to serve. You will need at least one caregiver for every two or three babies and toddlers. (Use the lower number for infants, the higher number for the oldest toddlers.) Always plan for at least two caregivers to work together in the nursery, no matter how few children are present.

Churches have a variety of options when choosing caregivers for VBS: paid workers, volunteer workers, youth helpers or a combination. Using paid caregivers has some advantages:

>> It creates higher expectations of a quality program.
>> It provides continuity of caregivers in the nursery each day.
>> It fosters dependability on the part of caregivers to be there promptly each day.
>> It provides more responsible supervision of volunteer caregivers.

Volunteer caregivers are more likely to view their job as a ministry and will not want to be paid. You may decide to have one paid caregiver and several volunteers; or if you have a dependable adult volunteer who wants the responsibility, you may be able to staff your nursery entirely with volunteers. The important thing is to make sure your lead caregiver is qualified and experienced. He or she should be prepared to arrive at least 15 minutes (or more if you have morning staff devotions) before VBS starts each day.

Playtime!

Babies and toddlers don't have to be taught to play. As soon as they are able, babies play—first with hands and fingers, then with human faces and easy-to-grasp toys. They grow to play simple games with adults, manipulate every object from a rock to the family dog in an endless round of activity that defines the way babies learn about and make sense of the world.

Play and exploration develop not only a baby's physical coordination but also the ability to think and reason, as well as language and social skills. When loving adults play with the baby, these skills are built even more effectively.

>> **Get on the floor!** On the floor, you are naturally at a baby's eye level. (This also means you get a baby's point of view on the world—be sure to take it in!)

>> **Begin yourself.** To interest a child in an activity (such as rolling a ball, playing peek-a-boo or building a block tower), begin doing the activity yourself.

>> **Talk with the baby as you play.** "Look, Jenny! Here is a blue block. I'm going to set it right here on this yellow block." Jenny might knock the blue block off the yellow one. "I see you knocked the blue block off, Jenny! It fell down. I'm putting the blue one on the yellow one again. . . ." You have just invented a game to play with Jenny.

>> **Build on the game.** For an older baby or toddler, you might expand the game by adding a red block, putting the blue block under the yellow one or hiding a block under a beanbag to see if Jenny will move the beanbag to find the block.

>> **Talk about God.** In your conversation, occasionally make brief comments to build an interest in God or Jesus. For example, while building with blocks, you might say, "God made your eyes to see the blue and yellow blocks."

>> **Know when not to interact or play with a baby.** Most children (even very young ones) will call to you or let you know when they would like some company and a little play. However, if the child is already occupied, exploring on his or her own, it's not necessary or even helpful to interrupt this valuable "playing alone" to interact. Talk about what you see the child doing ("You're really working hard to stack those blocks!") and resist the urge to give advice or a guiding hand. "Let me help you" should be reserved only for times when the child is becoming frustrated.

Tips for Playing with Young Babies:

>> Create a safe space for exploring (eliminate hazards and provide a variety of simple objects to explore).

>> Show and move interesting, colorful objects; talk to the baby about them as you do so.

>> Use the baby's name often.

>> Be sure there is enough for baby to do. Place objects to be explored nearby for hitting and grasping.

>> If a baby seems bored, provide different objects to explore, move baby to a different location (moving outside often works wonders!), play a short game with him or her, etc.

>> Try a hiding game (cover a ball with a blanket; ask, "Where's the ball, Meara?" then remove the blanket and say, "There's the ball!").

>> Sing to babies, making up spontaneous songs.

>> Let baby take the lead. Imitate his or her actions. Then add an action of your own to make it a game.

Tips for Playing with Older Babies and Toddlers:

>> Talk to and play with puppets and dolls. Include the child in the conversation, using his or her name.

>> Try more complex hiding games (invite the baby to point to the place where the hidden object is; play short, limited kinds of hide-and-seek games).

>> Explain how things happen ("You rolled the ball, Tyler. It went under the crib.")

>> Share in block play, etc. Talk about what you do, describing your actions and the child's reactions. Occasionally provide sand and water play for children, too.

>> Begin to ask questions such as "What do you think happened to the ball, Bryson?" Give the child adequate time to respond, and look for nonverbal answers.

Play and exploration are the most basic parts of any baby's day. YOUR thoughtful participation in play activities will enhance not only the child's learning, but your relationship with the child as well.

Teaching Tips

>> For younger toddlers and babies, the activities referred to should be used one-on-one and should continue as long as the child expresses interest. The child's learning, not maintaining a rigid schedule, should be the foremost consideration.

>> Depending on the age of the child, activities may need to be modified. For instance, instead of gluing items to a paper, children simply color the paper.

>> Because these young children learn well through repetition, there is one Bible verse for all five sessions.

>> The *Prekindergarten/Kindergarten Teaching Resources* includes a number of attractive posters to use in decorating. Also, read other ideas under "Decorating for the Early Childhood Classroom" on page 21 and adapt the ideas according to your facility and the ages of the children. (Coloring Murals, Wall Cutouts, Star Disco Light, Balloons, and Metallic Table Covers and Fringe Curtains are some of the decorating accessories available from Gospel Light.)

NURSERY AND TODDLER GUIDE

Planning a Schedule

Child care for nursery-aged children should be more than just babysitting. Considering that in the average VBS program, children are in the nursery or classrooms for more than three hours each day, an interesting schedule of activities is an absolute must. The goal of the curriculum on the following pages is to teach individually each baby and toddler through natural learning processes what he or she can begin to learn about God. Do not force a child to sit still or participate in any activity in which he or she is not interested. Below is a sample VBS nursery schedule for children two to three years. This sample schedule is also available on the *Director's Guide CD-ROM*. Follow it loosely and adapt it to fit your needs.

VBS Nursery Schedule

Time	Activity
8:30-9:00	Parents sign in and drop off children. Play soft music. Children enjoy independent play.
9:00-9:30	If appropriate, one or two caregivers take three-year-olds into Opening Assembly with other age groups. Children under three years continue independent play.
9:30-9:45	Bible Story. Puppet welcome time. Movement activities (stretching, finger play, copycat, etc.).
9:45-10:30	Bible Learning Activities. Also free play. Children choose their activities.
10:30-10:45	Snack.
10:45-11:15	Outdoor walk and play.
11:15-11:30	Circle Time. Lay a large blanket on the floor and have children sit on it. Bring a picture book (about animals, families, nature, etc.) to look at with children. Sing songs that involve movement with children.
11:30-11:55	Bible Learning Activities. Also free play. Children choose their activities.
11:55-12:00	Free play and cleanup.
12:00-12:15	Parents pick up children.

NURSERY AND TODDLER GUIDE

 Session One >> God Sends Jesus

Lesson Overview

Scripture
Luke 2:1-7

Bible Words
God loved us and sent his Son. (See 1 John 4:10.)

Lesson Focus
We can thank God for His love.

Bible Aims
During this session, each child may
1. **LISTEN** to a story about Jesus' birth;
2. **POINT** to people God loves;
3. **THANK** God for His love.

Bible Story

Materials Checklist
>> Bible
>> Life of Jesus Poster from *Prekindergarten/Kindergarten Teaching Resources*

Jesus Is Born
(Hold Bible open to Luke 2 as you expressively tell the story. Do motions as indicated. Point to appropriate picture on Life of Jesus Poster.)

A Long Trip
One day Joseph said to Mary, "We must go to Bethlehem. We must write our names in the king's book."(*Make writing motions*.) So Joseph and Mary packed for their trip and left for Bethlehem.

Mary probably rode on a donkey. Clippety-clop, clippety clop! (*Pat cupped hands against legs*.) The donkey's feet went clippety-clop against the rocks on the road. Joseph walked beside her.

It was almost time for Mary to have a baby. Mary and Joseph knew that this baby would be very special. This baby would be God's Son, Jesus.

No Room!
Soon it was almost nighttime. Mary must have been tired! (*Yawn and stretch*.) Finally they got to Bethlehem. But the city was FULL of people! There was no room for them anyplace. (*Shake head no*.) The innkeeper said that every room was full.

Jesus' Birth
So Mary and Joseph went to a stable where animals were kept. They slept on straw. (*Lean head on hands as if sleeping*.) There in the stable, in the quiet nighttime, baby Jesus was born.

Mary wrapped baby Jesus in warm clothes. Then she laid Him on soft hay in the manger. (A manger is a box where animals eat food.)

Mary and Joseph wanted to take good care of Jesus. Jesus is God's Son!

Conclusion
Mary and Joseph were glad that Jesus was born. We're glad that Jesus was born, too. God sent Jesus because He loves us. Let's thank God for His love. Pray, **Thank You, God, for loving** (name children). Lead children to point to each other as names are said aloud.

Session One >> Bible Learning Activities

Block Stable

Materials Checklist
>> masking tape
>> blocks
>> toy animals

Preparation: Use masking tape to outline a stable on the floor.

Procedure: Children stack blocks on masking-tape line to build a stable. Children play with animals in stable as you talk about today's Bible story. (Note: Remove masking tape immediately after use.)

Conversation: **Our Bible story today tells about a time Mary and Joseph stayed in a stable. (A stable is where farm animals sleep and eat.) God's Son, Jesus was born in a stable. Fiona, what animals do you think might have been in the stable with Mary and Joseph? Nathan, what sounds do those animals make? God sent Jesus to be born because God loves us.** Lead children in prayer, thanking God for His love and for sending Jesus.

Rhythm Sticks

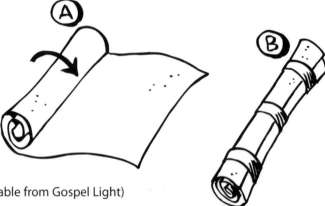

Materials Checklist
>> variety of colored construction paper
>> tape
>> markers
>> stickers (SonForce Assortment stickers available from Gospel Light)

Optional—
>> four 8-inch (20.5-cm) lengths of crepe paper for each child

Preparation: Make two rhythm sticks for each child, rolling and taping sheets of paper as shown in sketch. (Optional: Staple sticks at one end.)

Procedure: Demonstrate use of the rhythm sticks by tapping two sticks together. Give each child two sticks you prepared. Help children decorate them with markers and stickers. (Optional: tape crepe paper to one end of each stick.) Children tap rhythm sticks together as you say **God loves (Meara)**. Repeat, using the name of each child.

Conversation: **Madison, tap your rhythm sticks together. One, two, three, four. It's fun to tap our sticks! It's good to know that God loves us. He loves each and every one of us! That's why God sent His Son, Jesus.**

NURSERY AND TODDLER GUIDE

Session Two >> Shepherds Thank God for Jesus

Lesson Overview

Scripture
Luke 2:8-20

Bible Words
God loved us and sent his Son. (See 1 John 4:10.)

Lesson Focus
We can thank God for Jesus.

Bible Aims
During this session, the child may
1. **LISTEN** to a story about the shepherds who came to see baby Jesus;
2. **PRETEND** to be sheep and the shepherds who came to see baby Jesus;
3. **THANK** God for Jesus.

Bible Story

Materials Checklist
>> Bible
>> Life of Jesus Poster from *Prekindergarten/Kindergarten Teaching Resources*

Shepherds Visit Jesus
(Hold Bible open to Luke 2 as you expressively tell the story. Do motions as indicated. Point to appropriate picture on Life of Jesus Poster.)

A Few Shepherds
One quiet night a long time ago, some shepherds were outside taking care of their sheep.

All at once, the sky was full of bright light. (*Spread open hands.*) The shepherds looked up and saw an angel! The shepherds were very afraid.

Many Angels
But the angel said, "Do not be afraid. I have good news. God's Son, Jesus, has been born. (*Fold arms as if holding a baby.*) You can go see Him. He is in a stable, wrapped up warm and lying in a manger."

Then the sky was FULL of angels! The angels said, "Glory to God!" The angels were thanking God for sending Jesus.

Then the angels left. The shepherds said, "Let's go find this special baby. Let's hurry!" (*Make walking motions with fingers.*) Steppity-steppity-step—the shepherds hurried along the road until they found the stable where Jesus was.

One Baby
Baby Jesus was lying in a manger in a stable. Everything was just as the angel had said. The shepherds were so happy to see baby Jesus!

Then the shepherds started walking back to take care of their sheep. (*Make walking motions with fingers.*) Along the way, they told the good news to everyone they saw. "Jesus is born! Jesus is born!" The shepherds were glad Jesus was born!

Conclusion
The shepherds thanked God for sending Jesus to be born. We can thank God for sending Jesus to be born, too. Pray, **Thank You, God, for sending Jesus.**

Session Two >> Bible Learning Activities

Sheep Masks

Materials Checklist
- paper plates
- scissors
- cotton balls
- glue
- masking tape

Optional—
- construction paper

Preparation: For each child, cut the center out of a paper plate. Use masking tape to outline a large square on the floor to make a sheepfold.

Procedure: Children glue cotton balls to paper plate rims to make sheep masks. (Optional: Cut sheep ears from construction paper for children to glue to masks.) Children hold sheep masks in front of the faces and pretend to be sheep. Interested children may pretend to be shepherds and lead "sheep" into the masking-tape sheepfold to sleep for the night.

Conversation: **Our Bible story today tells about some shepherds. Shepherds take care of sheep. Wesley, would you like to pretend to be a shepherd? One night, the shepherds visited baby Jesus. They thanked God for Jesus!** Lead children in prayer, thanking God for sending Jesus.

Stable Life

Materials Checklist
- dolls
- doll blankets
- cardboard box

Optional—
- Bible-times costumes

Procedure: Children wrap dolls in blankets and place dolls in cardboard box to sleep in pretend mangers. (Optional: Children dress in Bible-times costumes.)

Conversation: **In our Bible story today, an angel told some shepherds to look for a special baby. The baby was in a stable, a place like a barn where animals sleep. Joleen, who was the baby born in a stable? The shepherds were glad when they saw baby Jesus. After they left the stable, they thanked God for sending Jesus to be born. We can thank God, too!** Pray, **Thank You, God, for sending Jesus to be born.**

NURSERY AND TODDLER GUIDE

Session Three >> Jesus Loves Children

Lesson Overview

Scripture
Luke 18:15-17

Bible Words
God loved us and sent his Son. (See 1 John 4:10.)

Lesson Focus
We can thank Jesus for His love.

Bible Aims
During this session, the child may
1. **LISTEN** to a story about how Jesus showed love for children;
2. **MAKE** facial expressions that show gladness for Jesus' love;
3. **THANK** Jesus for His love.

Bible Story

Materials Checklist
>> Bible
>> Life of Jesus Poster from *Prekindergarten/Kindergarten Teaching Resources*

Jesus Loves Children

(Hold Bible open to Luke 18 as you expressively tell the story. Do motions as indicated. Point to appropriate picture on Life of Jesus Poster.)

Getting Ready
One day, some parents heard that Jesus was coming. They wanted their children to meet Jesus! They must have washed the children's faces and combed the children's hair. (*Pretend to wash your face and comb your hair.*) The mothers probably made sure their children were wearing clean clothes. Then off the families went see Jesus.

Sending the Children Away
When they got to where He was, Jesus was talking to grown-ups. The mothers and fathers took their children by the hand and went around the crowd to be close to Jesus. They must have been happy and excited! (*Make a happy face.*)

But then, some of Jesus' friends said, "Stand back! Jesus is too busy to see children."

How sad the families must have felt! (*Make a sad face.*) They turned to walk away. But then Jesus said, "Let the children come to Me! Do not send the children away. I love children. I want to see them!"

Getting to See Jesus
Jesus' friends were surprised that Jesus cared so much about children. (*Make a surprised face.*) The children came to Jesus. Jesus put His arms around them. He prayed for each child. They must have felt very happy! (*Make a happy face.*) The children knew that Jesus loved them.

Conclusion
Jesus showed that He loved the children who came to see Him. Jesus was glad to see the children. Jesus loves each of you, too. Let's make happy faces to show how glad we are that Jesus loves us. Pray, **Thank You, Jesus, for loving us.**

NURSERY AND TODDLER GUIDE

Session Three >> Bible Learning Activities

Little Children

Materials Checklist
>> construction paper
>> scissors
>> glue
>> craft sticks
>> crayons or markers

Preparation: Cut construction paper into circles, triangles, squares and other geometric shapes. Glue shapes to craft sticks, making puppets.

Procedure: Children decorate puppets. Then they move puppets to act out Bible story action.

Conversation: **Candice, do you want your puppet to be Jesus or one of the children who came to see Him in today's Bible story? Jesus showed love to the children who came to see Him. Jesus loves ALL children. Jesus loves you!** Pray, **Thank You, Jesus, for loving . . .** Point to a child, leading the child to say his or her name. Repeat for each child.

City Blocks

Materials Checklist
>> blocks
>> toy people

Procedure: Children use blocks to build structures. Talk about the places they go (home, church, library, park, grocery store, mall, etc.). Children play with toy people.

Conversation: **Our city has many places we can build. Erin, where are some of the places you go? Jesus loves you when you are at the (park). Jesus loves you everywhere you go!**

NURSERY AND TODDLER GUIDE

 Session Four >> Jesus Helps a Sick Boy

Lesson Overview

Scripture
John 4:46-53

Bible Words
God loved us and sent his Son. (See 1 John 4:10.)

Lesson Focus
We can thank Jesus for helping us.

Bible Aims
During this session, the child may
1. **LISTEN** to a story about Jesus helping a sick boy;
2. **POINT** to pictures of people Jesus helps;
3. **THANK** Jesus for His help.

Bible Story

Materials Checklist
>> Bible

Jesus Helps a Sick Boy
(Hold Bible open to John 4 as you expressively tell the story. Do motions as indicated.)

A Sick Boy
Our Bible tells about a boy who was very sick. His father must have tried to take good care of his sick boy. But the boy did not get better. (*Shake head.*)

A Loving Father
How sad I am! thought the little boy's father. (*Frown.*) Then he remembered that Jesus made sick people well. *I must find Jesus,* the father thought. And off he went.

The father walked and walked. (*Walk in place.*) Finally he reached the town where Jesus was. Many people were listening to Jesus. (*Cup ear with hand.*) The father ran up to Jesus. "I have been looking for You, Jesus!" he cried. "My son is very sick. Please come, or he will die."

Some Good News
Jesus loved the man, and He loved the man's son. "You may go home," Jesus said. "Your son will live." The man was happy. (*Smile.*) He believed Jesus' words. He knew that Jesus' words were true.

The father began to walk home. (*Walk in place.*) While he was walking, he saw some people coming toward him. As they got closer, the father saw they were his helpers. "Sir, your son is well!" they told him. "He will live!"

"I know," the father said. "Jesus made him well." The man and his helpers were very happy. (*Smile.*) They were thankful for Jesus' love and help.

Conclusion
Jesus loved the boy and helped Him. Jesus loves us and will help us, too. Jesus helps us when we are sick. Jesus helps us no matter where we go. Lead children in prayer, thanking Jesus for helping us.

Session Four >> Bible Learning Activities

Hide and See

Materials Checklist
Optional—
>> doll

Procedure: Children cover their eyes while you invite a child or adult helper to hide (crouch behind a chair, stand behind a door, crawl under a table, etc.). Children uncover their eyes and then follow you as you lead them in looking for the hidden person. Repeat with different people hiding as time and interest permit. (Optional: Instead of having a person hide, hide a doll for children to look for.)

Conversation: **We are playing a game to remember our Bible story. We are looking for David just like the man in our story looked for Jesus. Beth, where do you think David is? In our story, Jesus showed love by helping the sick boy. Jesus helps us when we're sick, too. Jesus helps us because He loves us.** Lead children in prayer, thanking Jesus for His love and help.

Happy Faces

Materials Checklist
>> discarded magazines
>> scissors
>> marker
>> large sheet of butcher paper
>> glue

Preparation: Cut pictures of happy faces from magazines. Print "We are glad! Jesus helps us!" across the top of large sheet of paper.

Procedure: Children glue face pictures to the paper to make a collage. As children work, talk about the happy people in the Bible story.

Conversation: **In today's story, a father was happy. The father's helpers were happy. Hunter, why were the people happy? They were happy because Jesus helped them. Jesus helps people because Jesus loves them. Jesus loves you and He loves me and Jesus will always help us!** Pray, thank Jesus for His love and for helping the children in the class. Name each child as you pray.

NURSERY AND TODDLER GUIDE

 ## Session Five >> Jesus Is Alive

Lesson Overview

Scripture
Luke 2—24

Bible Words
God loved us and sent his Son. (See 1 John 4:10.)

Lesson Focus
We can thank God that Jesus is alive.

Bible Aims
During this session, the child may
1. **LISTEN** to a story about Jesus' friends when they saw that Jesus is alive;
2. **SHOW** gladness that Jesus is alive;
3. **THANK** God for His love and that Jesus is alive.

Bible Story

Materials Checklist
>> Bible
>> Life of Jesus Poster from *Prekindergarten/Kindergarten Teaching Resources*

Jesus Is Alive
(Hold Bible open to Luke 2 as you expressively tell the story. Do motions as indicated. Point to appropriate picture on Life of Jesus Poster.)

Jesus on Earth
When Jesus was here on Earth, Jesus did many wonderful things for people. He made blind people see. (*Open eyes wide.*) He made sick people well. (*Make walking motions with fingers.*) He taught people about God. Jesus loved people very much. Many people loved Him.

But not everyone loved Jesus. Some people hated Jesus. They wanted to hurt Jesus. Jesus let them take Him. Jesus died.

A Tomb in a Garden
Jesus' friends were very sad when Jesus died. (*Make a sad face.*) The sad friends put Jesus' body in a tomb in a garden. The tomb was a little room cut out of the side of a hill. Jesus' friends rolled a big stone in front of the opening of the tomb.

Later, some women walked to Jesus' tomb. The women were very sad. (*Make a sad face.*) But when they got to the tomb, the big stone in front of the tomb had been moved. (*Make a surprised face.*) Jesus' body was GONE.

An angel was there. "Jesus is not dead," the angel said. "He is alive!" NOW The women were so happy! (*Make a happy face.*) The women ran to share the happy news with Jesus' other friends. "Jesus IS alive!" they said. Now all of Jesus' friends were happy!

Conclusion
Jesus' friends were so glad when they saw that Jesus is alive. Jesus' friends knew how much Jesus loved them. Jesus loves us, too. We're glad that He is alive. Pray, **Thank You, God, for Your love and that Jesus is alive.**

Session Five >> Bible Learning Activities

Mirror Mirror

Materials Checklist
>> one or more large handheld unbreakable mirrors

Procedure: Demonstrate to children how to make a variety of faces: happy, sad, surprised, angry, scared, etc. Then, lead children in repeating, "Children, children, who do you see? I see a happy face looking at me!" Each child takes a turn to look in a mirror and make a happy face. Repeat rhyme several times, each time calling out a different kind of face to make. Briefly tell the Bible story and talk with children about the feelings of the people in the story.

Conversation: **Our Bible story today tells us that Jesus is alive. Emma, how do you think Jesus' friends felt when they heard that Jesus is alive? I'm glad that Jesus is alive! Travis, can you make a happy face?** Lead children in prayer, asking God for His help to obey Him.

Music Parade

Materials Checklist
>> *SonForce Kids CD* and player

Procedure: Play "SonForce Kids Theme" as you lead children in a parade around the room. As you walk, children recite with you, **One, two, three, four; Jesus is ALIVE!** Lead children in doing a variety of actions as you walk (wave arms, stomp feet, wiggle fingers, clap hands, etc.).

Conversation: **In today's Bible story, some women told Jesus' friends that Jesus is alive. This made Jesus' friends very happy! We show that we're happy Jesus is alive by having a parade and telling others the happy news that Jesus is alive.** Pray, **Dear God, thank You that Jesus is alive.**

PRETEEN ENRICHMENT IDEAS

THESE STUDENTS STRUGGLE TO FIT IN BETWEEN TEENS AND YOUNGER KIDS. FIND OUT HOW TO GET PRETEENS INVOLVED IN A MEANINGFUL WAY.

PRETEEN ENRICHMENT IDEAS

Teen Helpers

Teens make wonderful VBS helpers (see "Using Youth Helpers" beginning on p. 29). But what about fifth- through sixth-grade students, sometimes referred to as tweens? These students struggle to fit in between teens and younger students. When it comes to VBS, they'd like to be involved but might shy away from participating in a program that appears geared to younger kids. They're also too young to be effective helpers with first through fourth graders.

Suggestions for Customizing Your VBS

Use the *Preteen Bible Story Center Guide* and "Preteen Adaptation" ideas in the other *Center Guides* to choose and adapt learning activities for these students. The *Preteen Bible Story Center Guide* provides Optional Enrichment Verses for preteens. Also consider adding one or more of the following enrichment ideas:

>> Call the program for this age group by a different but similar name such as "KidForce Agency" or "Team SonForce." This name has obvious connections to the SonForce Kids VBS, but is set apart as well.

>> Arrange a time before VBS for students to design and make their own VBS T-shirts. Silk-screen, tie-dye and fabric paints are easy techniques for making custom shirts.

>> Also before VBS, arrange for students to help with VBS decorating. Students could be divided into teams, with each team assigned to help a different leader decorate his or her activity center. Or perhaps assign students a special area to decorate on their own: hallways, the assembly room, lobby area, etc. (Coloring Murals, Wall Cutouts, Star Disco Light, Balloons, and Metallic Table Covers and Fringe Curtains are some of the decorating accessories available from Gospel Light.)

>> Set up a tent or awning in an outdoor area for older students to use as a gathering place and/or Bible Story Center.

>> Get students involved in a service project at a local charitable organization or at the church in the morning, and have a fun outing in the afternoon. Afternoon outings could include bowling, skating, swimming, climbing walls or ropes courses, hiking, going on a scavenger hunt, etc.

>> Start later in the day, and run later in the afternoon.

>> Students make their own, more elaborate snacks: build-your-own sundaes, make-your-own pizzas, create-your-own trail mix, etc.

>> Divide students by gender for some sections of the lesson. You may find students more willing to share during the life-application segment of the lesson if they are in groups of the same gender. Even if you keep students together for the Bible story, separate them to work on the *SFA Manual*.

>> Before VBS begins, have a special session with the students during which they design their own logo. They can use the logo to make T-shirts and/or as part of decorations they create for their own classrooms.

>> Have special sessions for students to learn skills they can use elsewhere in the program. Students this age can learn to run light and sound boards during assemblies, use a computer to create graphics for word charts for songs, take pictures with a digital camera for computer slideshows, etc.

>> In place of one or more activity centers, have electives for preteens: cooking, volleyball—anything that might pique the interest of a preteen! Ask members of your church to prepare electives based on their interests and skills.

>> Students practice skits to perform for younger age levels. They may perform Bible-story or assembly skits from the *Assemblies and Skits Production Guide*.

>> If your group of students is small enough, select a few each day to be "stars" of the day. Interview them during assemblies and ask wacky questions or ask them to show off strange and unusual talents. Unless they are uncomfortable and don't want to participate, be sure to feature each student during the course of your VBS.

>> Be sure to take a lot of photographs and display them right away. You might consider sending them via e-mail to participating students.

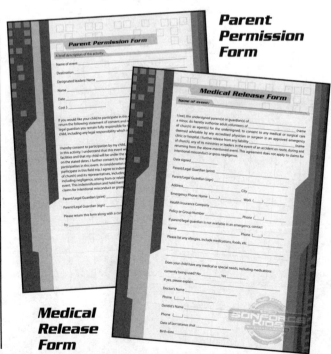

Parent Permission Form

Medical Release Form

INTERGENERATIONAL VBS GUIDE

AN INTERGENERATIONAL VBS OFFERS FAMILIES AN OPPORTUNITY TO GROW TOGETHER IN A FUN AND EXCITING FORMAT.

INTERGENERATIONAL VBS GUIDE

Bring Families Together

In today's busy, fragmented world, few families have regular opportunities to work, learn and laugh together. Even less common for most families are special times of exploring solid, practical guidance from God's Word for daily family living. An Intergenerational SonForce Kids VBS offers the families of your church and community an opportunity to grow together in a fun and exciting format. Instead of the traditional VBS, which may or may not involve adults, an Intergenerational VBS keeps family members together for part—or even all—of the activities. There are many ways to adapt your SonForce Kids materials to effectively involve families. For example, you may want to

» plan the Opening Assembly for families and then have family members go to their age-level groups (see Option A, p. 96)

» keep families together for the entire session (see Option B, p. 96)

Whichever approach you prefer, in these pages you'll find the help you need to make your Intergenerational SonForce Kids a success.

Family Groups

Assign each family to a group of four to six families (12 to 16 people). The number of family groups you form will depend on your total attendance, as well as the space and staff you have available. Let each family group choose their own name (Amazing Agents, Spectacular Spies, Star Agents, Team SonForce, etc.). Choose a distinctive color and symbol for each family group's name tags. (Name Tag Holders available from Gospel Light.)

Family Activity Centers

Determine which activities you will offer for family groups (Family Activity Centers) and which will be for age-level groups. We provide adaptations for families for the Theme Center, but you can adapt any of the other centers as well.

Set up activity centers as described in the Activity Center Guide on page 57. Family groups will rotate among Family Activity Centers and age-level activity centers according to a schedule you create.

Guides

Each family group should have one or more Guides (see p. 28) who lead the group to the appropriate centers. These Guides help families get to know each other better and assist parents in involving their children in activities.

Family Activity Center Leaders

Enlist at least one person to direct and/or teach each Family Activity Center. These friendly leaders remain at their centers and work with each group as it rotates through.

> **Note**
>
> The intergenerational approach is recommended for children ages four and up and their families. Younger children often find it difficult to participate effectively in a program where they are expected to rotate from center to center.

How It Works

The schedules and ideas on these pages show how an Intergenerational VBS can work in your church. Choose the option that fits your situation best and then adjust as needed.

Registration/Arrival

As families arrive, they are assigned to a permanent group, introduced to their Guide and are given or have the opportunity to make their group name tags.

Opening Assembly

The session begins as everyone meets together for the Opening Assembly, which includes a welcome, songs, a skit or other options (see *Assemblies and Skits Production Guide*). Below are suggestions to get all ages participating right from the start.

1. Prepare two or three families (or an entire family group) in advance to help teach a SonForce Kids song (including any motions);

2. Assign parts of songs to different family groups or

family members (dads, moms, all kids, dads and daughters, moms and sons, etc.); and/or

3. Invite a family from each group to participate in a simple stunt or contest that involves the whole family. Use a different stunt each day. See the stunts provided in the *Assemblies and Skits Production Guide* or use one of the examples below.
   >> Families race to dress a member of their group as a special agent, complete with black suit coat, hat and sunglasses, or as a robot using dryer hose and boxes;
   >> While seated and using only his or her feet, one member from each family races to write the Daily Mission on a large sheet of paper.
   >> Families compete in a water balloon toss, seeing how many times they can toss the balloon without breaking it;
   >> Families answer questions about the previous session's Bible story;
   >> Families race to put words of the session's Bible Memory Verse in the correct order.

After the Opening Assembly

Guides lead their family groups to the Family Activity Centers and other centers according to your chosen schedule. Use as many centers as your schedule and facilities allow. Have a predetermined signal to indicate when it is time to rotate to the next center (see suggested transition ideas in "Bonus Ideas" on p. 10).

Family Activity Center: Special Mission Pack

Families work together to fill a cardboard briefcase with activities family members complete.

Session 1—In Brief

Before class, photocopy Cardboard Briefcase Instruction Sheet (p. 94); enlarge and photocopy Cardboard Briefcase patterns (p. 95) onto card stock, making a set of patterns and an instruction sheet for each family. Families work together to assemble and decorate briefcases.

Instruct each family to come up with a name for their team of special agents and write it on their cardboard briefcase. Then, each family member chooses a special-agent name. Pass out index cards and ask each person to write their special-agent name on the card to make an ID badge. Punch holes in badges and attach

lengths of yarn so that badges can be worn around necks. Set aside a place in classroom for briefcases so that each day families can add items made during the session.

Session 2—Go-Go Gadgets

Families work together using art materials (beads, wire, aluminum foil, CDs, bottle caps, various PVC pipes and fittings, small machine parts, paper-towel tubes, old watches, nuts and bolts, plastic tubing, funnels, construction paper, newspaper, etc.) and recyclable materials (craft sticks, soda cans, cardboard, string, etc.) to design and create prototypes of gadgets that can be used to help others. They use wire, rubber bands, tape, low-temperature glue guns and staplers to put gadgets together. Place small gadgets into cardboard briefcases. Display larger gadgets in classroom.

Session 3—Object Observation

Each family member draws a picture of a favorite object on an index card. Next, families place cards face up in rows on the table. Family members look at objects for 20 seconds. Then, one member collects cards, shuffles cards, removes one card and places others face up on table. First person to identify the missing card gets a point. Continue playing until everyone has a chance to be the dealer. Then, each person draws another object and adds it to the other cards and play resumes as before. When time is up, gather cards, secure with a rubber band and place in cardboard briefcase. (Optional: Hold up Observation Poster from *Elementary Teaching Resources*. Show the appropriate side for the age level of the majority of the children in attendance. After 10 seconds, hide poster. Family members write down as many items from the poster as they remember. Repeat process, increasing time to study poster by 10-second increments as time and interest allow.)

Alternate Idea Family members make two drawings of the same object. Family members use cards to play Concentration.

Session 4—Secret Messages

Choose some or all of the invisible ink recipes below and set up one or more stations for each recipe, depending on the number of families and the number of different invisible-ink recipes offered. Write each recipe selected on a separate index card and place at the station.

Families rotate among stations, experimenting with the techniques by writing messages on pieces of scrap paper. Choosing their favorites, family members use the writing technique to write the invisible-ink recipe.

When finished, families collect their recipes and finished messages. They place them inside a manila envelope and put in cardboard briefcase. (Optional: Families stamp or write "Top Secret" on front of envelopes.)

Baking Soda Ink

Place purple grape-juice concentrate and several paintbrushes into a cup. Mix equal parts water and baking soda in a bowl. Dip toothpick or cotton swab into mixture and write message. Allow the ink to dry. To reveal the message, paint over it with juice concentrate.

Invisipics

Write your message with a blue crayon and then color over it with a red crayon. Use other crayons to draw a picture around the red area. To read the message, lay red acetate on top of the red area. (Hint: Transparent plastic folders are a great source of red acetate.)

White Messages

Use a white crayon to write a message. Color over the message with a marker to reveal the message.

Session 5—Message Missions

Choose some or all of the message-sending techniques below and set up one or more stations for each technique, depending on the number of families and the number of stations offered.

Families rotate among stations, practicing the techniques to send messages to other family members or to other families. After families have had a chance to try each station, they choose their favorite message-sending technique, write instructions and gather any materials that may still be available. Instructions and materials are placed in cardboard briefcase.

Cross-a-Message

Photocopy blank crossword puzzles from a newspaper or crossword puzzle book. On a sheet of paper write "Write in the empty boxes so that message looks like a simple crossword puzzle has been completed. Fill in any extra boxes with random letters." Tape instruction paper to table. Place pencils on table. At each station, set out scissors, scrap paper and pencils.

Pop-a-Message

Set out balloons, scrap paper and pencils. On a sheet of paper write, "Write messages on scrap paper and slip them inside balloons. Inflate balloons. Tap balloons back and forth a few times before popping to retrieve message inside." Tape instruction paper to table. (Tip: To pop balloons quietly, snip the necks with scissors.)

Fly-a-Message

Set out scissors, sheets of paper and pencils. On a sheet of paper write, "Write messages on sheets of paper. Fold paper to make an airplane. Then fly messages back and forth a few times before unfolding to read message." Tape instruction paper to table.

Reveal-a-Message

Set out magazines and Blacklight Pens (available from Gospel Light). On a sheet of paper write, "Use the pen to write a message over a magazine story. Use the light in the pen's cap to reveal your message." Tape instruction paper to table.

Create-a-Message

In addition to scissors, scrap paper and pencils, provide tape, string, paper clips, potato chip cans and other art and/or recyclable materials for families to develop their own method of passing messages. (For example: A family member ties a paper clip to one end of string and tucks other end inside his or her shoe. He or she attaches message to paper clip and begins to walk. Another family member comes up behind first one and steps on the message. First family member continues walking as second one bends down, pretends to tie shoe and retrieves message.)

Crafts

The *Special Agent Crafts for Kids* has a wide variety of craft ideas, including many that easily lend themselves to being done as a family project rather than as an individual one. (You may prefer to have crafts done in age-level groups.)

Recreation/Snacks

The *Recreation and Snack Center Guide* contains a good selection of snack ideas that allows families to work together in preparing and enjoying some tasty treats. The leader for this center provides the snack supplies and instructions; then families do the rest. If you need additional activities to fill this time, lead families in playing one of the recreation games described in *Recreation and Snack Center Guide*. (You may prefer to do these activities in age-level groups.)

Bible Story/Life Application

The leader in charge of the Bible Story Center presents each day's story from the *Middler Bible Story Center Guide* to each family group. To help families talk about ways that the Bible story applies to them today, read the student *SFA Manuals*. Prepare some questions and/or activities for each family group to work on together and some for each family to work on separately. Another option to reinforce the Bible lesson is using the Bible Story Review Game or Memory Verse Game in the *Bible Games Center Guide*.

To keep the attention of the various age levels present during the story time, consider these ideas:

>> Arrange seating in a wide semicircle to avoid having any of the younger students in the back. Families should sit together so that parents can help their children focus on the story presentation.

>> Keep the story time brief. With four- and five-year-olds in the group, a story should not exceed five minutes.

>> Instead of telling story, perform skits instead. Ahead of time, assign a Bible Story Skit (available in *Assemblies and Skits Production Guide*) to one or more families. Each day a different skit is performed by the adults and older children of the assigned families.

If you choose to do part of the session in age-level groups, students may complete activities in appropriate age-level *SFA Manuals* to review story and application. Parents may then enjoy engaging in the recommended adult Bible study, *Wired That Way*.

Closing

All family groups and activity center leaders meet together to conclude each session with singing, Bible Memory Verse review and an invitation to the next session. Guides collect name tags and help families gather crafts and other items to be taken home.

Teaching Tips

Most of your team members and attending families are likely to have only limited experience with family group activities. Family groups that have a wide range of age levels pose some unique challenges for those who are less familiar with the dynamics of a mixed-age group. A few helpful guidelines for teaching family groups are presented below.

>> Use a signal to get everyone's attention before you speak. Blowing a whistle, sounding a musical note, ringing a bell, quickly flashing the lights off and on, or making a large gesture (holding both arms straight overhead) are all effective ways to get attention without shouting. Explain your signal and practice it several times with the group. Ask the students to help their parents learn to respond to your signal.

>> Talk to all age groups. If a leader focuses on the four-year-olds, older students and adults will tune out. If a leader focuses on the parents, the students will get restless. Remember, even four-year-olds can understand over 90 percent of normal adult conversation. The following tips can help you talk to all age groups:

1. Be brief, keep sentences short, use ample gestures and facial expressions, and vary the pitch and volume of your voice.

2. Intentionally refer to different age and grade levels, as well as specific families, in your talk. ("I bet the third graders already figured that out." Or "Daniel couldn't get a hamburger at a restaurant the way you can, Jeff.") When you need to say something specifically to parents, you may ask the students to cover their ears because you want to tell their parents a secret. Of course, the kids will suddenly become highly attentive!

>> Enlist parents as partners in "crowd control." Many parents who are perfectly capable

of controlling their children in normal situations will abdicate that responsibility when someone else is the leader. And many leaders are reluctant to deal with a behavior problem when the parents are present. Explain to parents that in a group family-learning situation, parents and leaders must take joint responsibility for guiding children. For example say, "Because there are lots of people and lots of activities, it is not always possible for a parent or leader to see everything. We must help each other in giving good directions and enforcing limits so that we can all have a relaxed, enjoyable time together."

>> When families are working together, encourage parents to allow their children to do as much of the work as possible. Because of the variance in students' age levels, some parents will need to do more "helping" than others. Remind parents that the goal is not to see which family produces the most attractive project or wins in a game or activity. The goal is for families to enjoy working and learning together.

>> When families are given a question to discuss, instruct parents to share brief answers and experiences that encourage children to participate. Lengthy explanations or stories tend to stifle children's interest, so parents should keep their comments as concise as possible.

>> Provide an opportunity for families to pray together during the Bible story part of the session. Instruct parents to keep the prayers very simple so that even the youngest child can participate fully. You may suggest the following helpful approaches, which can also aid parents who are uncomfortable with praying aloud:

1. Let a family member suggest one thing to pray about; then each family member offers a one-sentence prayer of agreement about that. ("I'm glad Molly is thankful for our family.")

2. Invite each family member to tell God one thing for which he or she is thankful or to ask Him for one thing.

3. Each family member thanks God for the family member to his or her right.

4. One family member volunteers to pray; then they all join in saying "amen" ("so be it" or "let it be done") at the end.

Cardboard Briefcase Instruction Sheet

1. Cut out pattern labeled "Inside of briefcase." Cut on all solid lines; fold on all dotted lines.

2. Glue sides together to form accordion folds, creating a large envelope.

3. Cut out pattern labeled "Briefcase cover." Decorate with the name of your special-agent team.

4. Place inside of briefcase in cover. Glue bottom and center of each side of the inside as indicated on pattern. Press firmly to set.

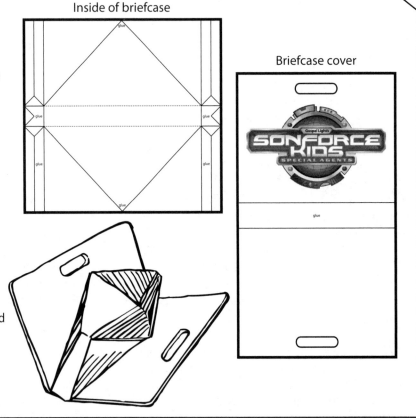

INTERGENERATIONAL VBS GUIDE

Cardboard Breifcase Patterns

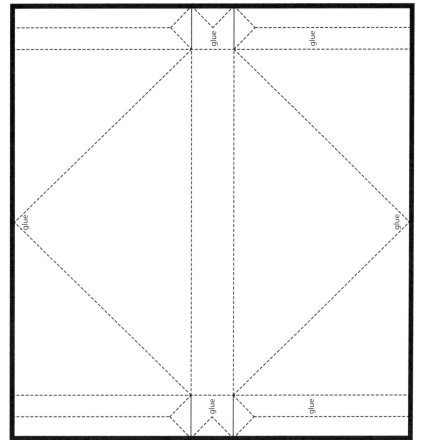

Inside of briefcase

Briefcase cover

These patterns are available as full-size electronic files on the *Director's Guide* CD-ROM.

95

© 2007 GOSPEL LIGHT. PERMISSION TO PHOTOCOPY GRANTED. SONFORCE KIDS *DIRECTOR'S GUIDE*

INTERGENERATIONAL VBS GUIDE

Intergenerational VBS Schedule Option A:
Family Opening, Family Activity Plus Separate Age-Level Activities

Sample 90- to 120-Minute Schedule

Time	Children	Parents
15 Minutes	Opening Assembly	Opening Assembly
20-30 Minutes	Family Activity Center	Family Activity Center
40-60 Minutes	Age-Level Groups for Snacks, Games, Bible Story Center	Adult Bible Study, *Wired That Way*
15 Minutes	Closing Assembly	Closing Assembly

Intergenerational VBS Schedule Option B:
All Family

Sample 90- to 120-Minute Schedule

Time	Group 1	Group 2	Group 3
15 Minutes	Opening Assembly	Opening Assembly	Opening Assembly
20-30 Minutes	Family Activity Center	Recreation/Snack	Bible Story Center
20-30 Minutes	Recreation/Snack	Bible Story Center	Family Activity Center
20-30 Minutes	Bible Story Center	Family Activity Center	Recreation/Snack
15 Minutes	Closing Assembly	Closing Assembly	Closing Assembly

Notes
1. Suggested times in each block include five minutes of transition time between activities.
2. Children under four years old remain in a separate area, following their own program schedule.
3. If you form more family groups than shown on these charts, two or more groups can be doing the same activity at the same time in different areas or rooms. Except for the Opening and Closing Assemblies, avoid grouping too many people together for any of the activities. Participation of each person will be greatest and potential behavior problems minimized when family groups are kept to four to six families (12 to 16 people).

BACKYARD BIBLE SCHOOL GUIDE

A BACKYARD BIBLE SCHOOL WORKS BECAUSE KIDS LOVE TO BE INVITED INTO A NEIGHBOR'S HOME WITH ALL THEIR FRIENDS.

BACKYARD BIBLE SCHOOL GUIDE

What It Is

Backyard Bible School is similar to traditional Vacation Bible School, but a backyard location affords some unique merits:

>> It provides a welcoming place close to home for unchurched children to learn about Jesus.

>> It enables Christians to minister within their own neighborhoods.

A Backyard Bible School works because kids love to be invited into a neighbor's home with all their friends. They enjoy the relaxed setting because it's a "come as you are" affair where bare feet and play clothes are the usual attire. The parents are happy because their children will be busy for over two hours. The home offers a special hospitality and proximity that is often not possible in a church setting. Also consider locations such as a local park, community center or an apartment-complex meeting room.

Note

You may wish to have parents sign a permission form and medical release form (see p. 88).

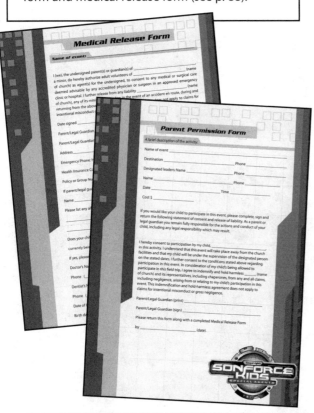

These forms are available as full-size, color electronic files on the *Director's Guide* CD-ROM.

Facilities

The home need not be large, but it should have a few basics:

>> a place to tell the story, such as a family room, patio or shaded lawn;

>> a separate place to do crafts, such as a patio, garage or basement (a table or two in this area is a good idea but not necessary; students can work while standing at the table, or they can work on the floor);

>> a place for serving refreshments (this can be the same area as used for crafts, but use separate table coverings for each activity);

>> a place to play active games such as a front yard, backyard or driveway (if necessary, a nearby park or common area will do).

Note: Be prepared to provide bathrooms for children to use.

How It Works

It begins with a Christian family making its home available for a given week(s). Then a leader and at least two adult or youth helpers join to make up a teaching team. They study and prepare the SonForce Kids learning materials.

Monday comes as usual, but this week will be very special. The members of the teaching team arrive early for prayer. The host family has prepared snacks and sent out a few kids with an adult helper to "round up the gang." The morning will include a Bible story with life application, Scripture memorization, songs, crafts, refreshments and games. Many students will hear about Jesus for the first time. Many will become Christians.

The Staff

The Host Family

It can't be done without a host family. This home is the focal point of all activity; the church is the resource, and the neighborhood is the mission field.

The natural hospitality and friendliness of the host family established among the neighbors will ensure good attendance. If the host family is new in the neighborhood, this will be an opportunity to meet neighbors and establish rapport.

The specific responsibilities of the host family are

1. to invite the other teaching team members to its home a week ahead of time to look over the facilities and make plans;
2. to give out the invitations to neighborhood families;
3. to have the home in order;
4. to plan and serve the refreshments;

The Leader

The leader's influence is primary in the lives of the students. Therefore his or her spirit, knowledge of the subject matter and knowledge of how to deal with students will either "make or break" the week for everyone else involved. It is the leader's job to take the reins as the first student arrives. The leader's smile and friendly, decisive directions will help each student feel wanted, happy and cooperative. The helpers are available to do the jobs that the leader delegates to them. When the leader is able to encourage a spirit of love and cooperation among the students, as well as the mutual respect of all involved, this spirit lives on in the minds of the students—even years later.

The leader's specific responsibilities are

1. to know what is scheduled to happen next;
2. to learn the Bible story and present it to the students;

3. to delegate or lead other activities such as crafts, recreation games and singing;
4. to lead the planning meeting at the home of the host family.

The Helpers

In most cases two helpers are needed. If more than 20 students are expected, enlist at least one more helper. A helper can be anyone with a love for children and a willing spirit. Teenagers and grandparents alike enjoy helping. Some helpers may have special abilities or interests in songs, crafts or recreation games.

It is important for helpers to show their personal interest by participating with the students. They should talk with students as they arrive and learn their names. Helpers need to guide students in the learning activities, sing with them, play games with them and enjoy the story with them. The helpers may be assigned to participate in the SonForce Kids skits. The general rule for helpers is to follow the directions of the leader in charge. However, the leader may ask a helper to lead an activity.

A helper's specific responsibility begins at the meeting in the home of the host family and then will depend on the specific jobs assigned by the leader.

BACKYARD BIBLE SCHOOL GUIDE

Personalize and adapt this calendar according to your own church's needs. Customizable files of this calendar are available on the *Director's Guide CD-ROM*. The items listed are suggestions to get you started.

Backyard Bible School Calendar

12 Weeks: >> Order course supplies.

8 Weeks: >> Educate the congregation with write-ups in bulletin or newsletter.

4 Weeks: >> Enlist a host family, leader and two (or more) helpers.
>> Set the dates, time and place of the Backyard Bible School.

3 Weeks: >> Make up a kit of materials (give appropriate **Center Guides** and **Helper Handbooks** to center teams).

2 Weeks: >> Host family member calls the team to schedule the meeting at the host family home the next week.
>> Leader prepares to delegate responsibilities at the meeting.

1 Week: >> Team meets at the home of the host family. Leader delegates responsibilities.
>> Team members prepare for their parts.

Backyard Bible School Sample Schedule

20-30 Minutes	Team Devotions and Preparation
10 Minutes	Opening Assembly
20-30 Minutes	Bible Story and Life Application
20-30 Minutes	Bible Games Center or Theme Center
20-30 Minutes	Recreation/Snack
20-30 Minutes	Crafts
10 Minutes	Closing

APPENDICES

>> **DIRECTOR'S GUIDE INDEX**
>> **PRODUCT INDEX**
>> **VBS QUESTIONNAIRE**

INDEX

Director's Guide Index

Activity Center Guide 57
Assemblies 40, 59
Backyard Bible School Guide 97
Child Abuse 41
Church Events 34, 44
Closing Program 50
Course Description 9
Course Overview 6
Curriculum Ordering Guide 8
Director's Calendar 22
Early Childhood VBS 20
Evangelism 35
Field Trips 44
Follow-Up 36
Intergenerational VBS Guide 89
Learning Plans 19
Materials: Preview 14
    Director's Sample Pack 14
    Music & Skit Production Pack 16
    Starter Kit 14
    Super Decorating & Resource Pack 16
    Super Starter Pack 16
Medication 88
Missions and Service Center Guide 63
Newsletters 55
Nursery and Toddler Guide 73
Planning 18
Preteen Enrichment Ideas 87
Preview Event 45
Publicity 34, 51
Publicity Calendar 54
Publicity Guide 51
Publicity Materials 53
Questionnaire 103
Recruiting 26
Safety 39
Special Events 43
Staff Job Descriptions 27
Step-by-Step Planning Guide 17
Theme: Bonus Theme Ideas 10
Theme: Set the Atmosphere 9
Training Volunteers 31
    VBS Format 18
    Youth Helpers 29

Product Index

Assemblies: *Assemblies and Skits Production Guide*
Certificates: *Reproducible Resources*, Student Certificate, Volunteer Certificate
Clip Art: *Clip Art & Publicity CD-ROM, Reproducible Resources*, Clip Art Sheet (Also available at www.gospellight.com and www.myvbs.com.)
Closing Program: *Assemblies and Skits Production Guide*
Clothing: Iron-On T-Shirt Transfer, SonForce Kids T-Shirt
Coloring Books/Pages: *God Helps Me Obey* coloring book, *Reproducible Resources*
Crafts: *Special Agent Crafts for Kids*
Decorating: *Preview DVD, Reproducible Resources*, Daily Mission Pennants
Evangelism and Discipling Booklets: *God Loves You! Growing as God's Child*
Games: *Bible Games Center Guide, Recreation and Snack Center Guide*
Gifts: Bookmark, Peel 'n Press Stickers, Skin Decals, Theme Buttons, Photo Frame
Missions Information: *Director's Guide, Preview DVD*
Music Center Activities: *SonForce Kids Songbook*
Music: *SonForce Kids Songbook, SonForce Kids CD, Leader's Music CD, Student Music Packs*
Organizational Helps: Attendance Chart, Name Tag, Plastic Tote Bag
Posters: *Teaching Resources*, Coloring Contest Flyer, Theme Posters
Prizes: Bookmark, Peel 'n Press Stickers, Skin Decals, Theme Buttons, Photo Frame
Promotional Items: Bulletin Cover/Insert or Promotional Flyer, Doorknob Hanger, Invitation Postcard (e-postcards available at www.myvbs.com), Promotional Radio Spots on SonForce Kids CD
Promotional Radio Spots: *SonForce Kids CD*
Puppets: Gadget Puppet, *Assemblies and Skits Production Guide, Reproducible Resources*
Recruiting: *Director's Guide, Preview DVD*
Skits: *Assemblies and Skits Production Guide, The Asteroid Incident Skit DVD*
Snacks: *Recreation and Snack Center Guide*
Song Motions: *SonForce Kids Songbook DVD*
Sound Effects: *SonForce Kids CD*
Split-Track Recording: *SonForce Kids CD*
Student Guides: *SFA Manuals*
Teaching Aids: *Bible Story Center Guides, Teacher's Guide, Teaching Resources*
Teaching Manual (Prekindergarten, Kindergarten): *Teacher's Guide*
Teaching Manual (Primary, Middler, Preteen): *Bible Story Center Guides*
Theme-related activities: *Director's Guide, Theme Center Guide*
Training: *Director's Guide, Helper Handbook*
Visual Aids: See Teaching Aids

VBS QUESTIONNAIRE

We'd Like to Know What You Think

After VBS is over, would you please take a few moments to complete this questionnaire? Once you're finished, fold it over so that the address side is on the outside and just drop it in the mail. Thank you!

Your name _____

Your title _____
      Staff/Volunteer (circle one)

Church name _____

Pastor's name _____

Church address _____

City, State, Zip _____

Denomination _____

Average weekly church attendance _____

Church fax (_____) _____

Church e-mail address _____

The optional information below will help us meet your needs.

How many Christian books do you buy each year? _____

1. How did you first learn about Gospel Light's SonForce Kids Vacation Bible School?

❏ Sunday School convention   ❏ Friend told me
❏ Phone call from Gospel Light   ❏ Brochure in mail
❏ Internet   ❏ VBS workshop
❏ Christian bookstore   ❏ Magazine advertisement
❏ Other (please specify) _____

2. Please tell us how you choose a VBS curriculum. On a scale of 1 to 4, rate each of the criteria listed below. (1=least important; 4=most important)

IMPORTANCE	LEAST			MOST
Bible content	1	2	3	4
Provides gospel presentation	1	2	3	4
Theme	1	2	3	4
Creative/captures imagination	1	2	3	4
Different from other courses	1	2	3	4
Center Guides content/format	1	2	3	4
Teaching resources	1	2	3	4
Music	1	2	3	4
Student guide content/format	1	2	3	4
Director's materials to organize program and recruit team members	1	2	3	4
Craft book	1	2	3	4
Skits	1	2	3	4
Cost/value	1	2	3	4
Promotional helps	1	2	3	4
Different from regular Sunday School curriculum	1	2	3	4
Other _____	1	2	3	4

3. Below are several statements about SonForce Kids. Please indicate how much you agree with each statement and also include your comments. If the statement does not apply to you, please circle N/A. (1=disagree strongly; 4=agree strongly)

	DISAGREE			AGREE	
N/A	1	2	3	4	I liked the Bible theme based on Joshua 1:9. _____
N/A	1	2	3	4	Kids of all ages enjoyed SonForce Kids. _____
N/A	1	2	3	4	The activities in the Bible Games Center and/or Theme Center were effective in reinforcing the Bible lesson. _____
N/A	1	2	3	4	The lesson format was easy to use. _____
N/A	1	2	3	4	Each Bible story and application was relevant to kids' lives. _____
N/A	1	2	3	4	Children enjoyed learning from the student guides. _____
N/A	1	2	3	4	The *Teaching Resources* visual aids were colorful and helped the children understand each Bible story.
N/A	1	2	3	4	Each day's skit helped children understand the lesson. _____
N/A	1	2	3	4	*Special Agent Crafts for Kids* had many fun, useful ideas. _____
N/A	1	2	3	4	SonForce Kids songs were fun, catchy and appropriate. _____
N/A	1	2	3	4	*Director's Guide* made organizing VBS easier. _____
N/A	1	2	3	4	*Reproducible Resources* contained many helpful resources. _____
N/A	1	2	3	4	The theme posters appealed to adults and children. _____
N/A	1	2	3	4	The T-shirt iron-on was attractive and worked well. _____

VBS QUESTIONNAIRE

4. What would you like to add, change or omit from Gospel Light's Vacation Bible School materials? _____
_____

5. Approximately how many children attended your VBS this year?
_____

6. How many years has your church used Gospel Light's VBS?
❏ First year ❏ 2 years ❏ 3 years
❏ 4 years ❏ 5+ years

7a. Who in your church decides which VBS curriculum to purchase?
❏ Pastor ❏ Minister of Education
❏ Children's Director ❏ Committee ❏ VBS Director

b. Please explain the process by which your church chooses VBS curriculum. (For example, if by committee, give titles of those involved.)
_____
_____

8. How did you schedule your VBS program? (Please check all that apply.)
❏ 5 consecutive days ❏ 2 consecutive weeks
❏ 5 consecutive evenings
❏ Other (please explain) _____

9. What teaching format did you use for elementary students?
❏ Self-contained classroom format ❏ Activity Center format
❏ Modified Activity Center format ❏ Intergenerational VBS
❏ Backyard Bible School
❏ Other (please explain) _____

10. After using Gospel Light's VBS this year, would you consider using Gospel Light again next year? ❏ Yes ❏ No

11. What theme would you most like to see Gospel Light develop for a future VBS curriculum? _____

12. What Bible content would you most like to see Gospel Light develop for a future VBS curriculum? _____

13a. What children's Sunday School curriculum does your church use? _____

b. How long have you been using your current Sunday School curriculum?
❏ Less than 1 year ❏ 2-3 years ❏ 4-5 years ❏ 5+ years

c. What is the approximate total attendance for all your Sunday School classes?
❏ Less than 50 ❏ 51-100 ❏ 101-200
❏ 201-300 ❏ 300+

14. Where do you usually buy your Christian education supplies?
❏ Bookstore
❏ Denominational supplier
❏ Curriculum publisher
❏ Other (please specify) _____

❏ Yes, I want to review Gospel Light's Sunday School Curriculum. Please send free samples for the following age levels:
❏ 2- & 3-year-olds ❏ 4- & 5-year-olds
❏ Grades 1 & 2 (Primary) ❏ Grades 3 & 4 (Middler)
❏ Grades 5 & 6 (Preteen)

Please send information about:
❏ Gospel Light Youth Curriculum
❏ Gospel Light Adult Curriculum

❏ Yes, I would like to be one of the first to preview VBS 2008!
Email _____

While we regret that we are unable to individually reply to the many survey responses we get each year, we want you to know that all feedback is read and considered by our editorial staff.

Thank you again for your comments.
Please fold form so that the address below is on the outside, tape to secure and drop in the mail.

---------- FOLD ----------

No postage necessary if mailed in the United States

BUSINESS REPLY MAIL
FIRST-CLASS MAIL PERMIT 51 VENTURA, CA
POSTAGE WILL BE PAID BY ADDRESSEE

Gospel Light
P.O. BOX 3875
Ventura, CA 93006

Attn: Children's Curriculum/VBS and Resources